W9-ACA-428

McGRAW-HILL

SCIENCE

Macmillan/McGraw-Hill Edition

Reading in Science Resources

GRADE 5

Mc Graw Hill **Macmillan McGraw-Hill**
New York   Farmington

Macmillan/McGraw-Hill

A Division of The **McGraw·Hill** *Companies*

Published by Macmillan/McGraw-Hill, of McGraw-Hill Education, a division of The McGraw-Hill Companies, Inc.,
Two Penn Plaza, New York, New York 10121. Copyright © by Macmillan/McGraw-Hill. All rights reserved.
The contents, or parts thereof, may be reproduced in print form for non-profit educational use with
McGraw-Hill Science, provided such reproductions bear copyright notice, but may not be reproduced in any form for
any other purpose without the prior written consent of The McGraw-Hill Companies, Inc., including, but not
limited to, network storage or transmission, or broadcast for distance learning.

Printed in the United States of America
ISBN 0-02-280171-5 / 5
5 6 7 8 9 024 06 05 04 03

Table of Contents

©Macmillan/McGraw-Hill

Plants and Their Parts

In the Ideas Circle below, plant parts are shown in the boxes on the top. Things plants do to survive are shown in the boxes on the bottom. Draw an arrow from the name of a plant part to one way the part helps the plant survive.

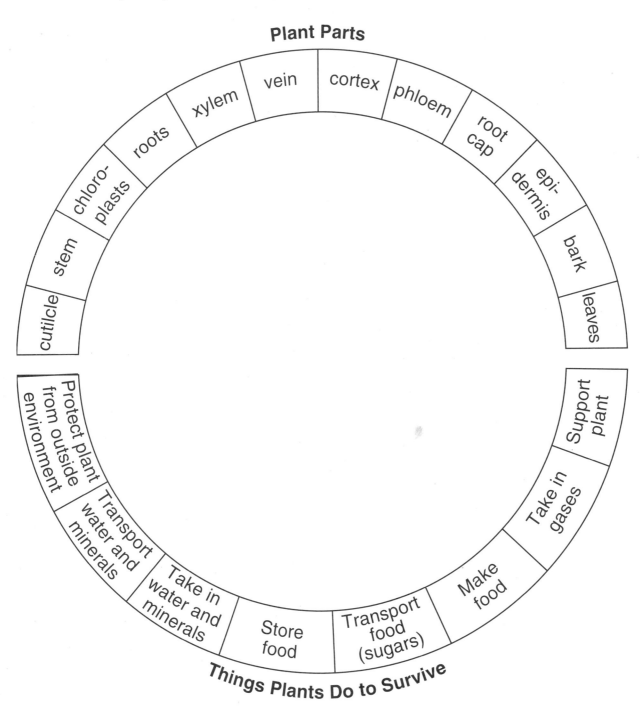

Plant Parts

vein · cortex · xylem · phloem · roots · root cap · chloroplasts · epidermis · stem · bark · cutilicle · leaves

Support plant · Take in gases · Make food · Transport food (sugars) · Store food · Take in water and minerals · Transport water and minerals · Protect plant from outside environment

Things Plants Do to Survive

©Macmillan/McGraw-Hill

Draw Conclusions

When you draw a conclusion, you decide if something is true. To do that , you need all the facts. Sometimes you have them, but sometimes you don't. Then you can't draw a conclusion.

Read the first four sets of facts below. Can you draw conclusions? Circle your answers. Read the last two sets of facts and write your answers.

1. Dad bought some beautiful plants. Thay have aerial roots that never touch the ground! They take in moisture and food from the air! Did Dad buy orchids?

   yes   no   not enough facts

2. All green plants have chlorophyll to help tham make food. Ivy is a green plant. Does ivy have chlorophyll?

   yes   no   not enough facts

3. Citrus fruit grows in places that have warm weather all year long. Does citrus fruit grow in Alaska?

   yes   no   not enough facts

4. Andy is taller than his brother Mark, but shorter than his brother Kevin. Kimberly is Andy's sister. Is she taller than Mark, too?

   yes   no   not enough facts

5. Sabrina graduated from high school two years before her cousin Raquel. Raquel's older brother, Hector, graduated one year before Sabrina.

   a. If Raquel graduated in 1999, what year did Sabrina graduate?

   _____.

   b. What year did Hector graduate? _____.

6. Eliot's dog, Rascal, is six years older than Molly's dog, Duffy. Vivian's dog, Sundance, is eight years younger than Rascal.

   a. If Duffy is 7, how old is Rascal? _____.

   b. How old is Sundance? _____.

What's the Verdict?

When you draw a conclusion, it's like solving a mystery. You are given a set of facts, or clues. If you put the facts together, you solve the mystery! **Read each set of clues, or facts, in the boxes below. Then really draw your conclusions on the spaces provided!**

I'm part of a plant. I fall off deciduous trees. On a ginkgo, I'm fan-shaped. What am I?	I have gymnosperm seeds in me. People often plant me and use me for winter decorations. What am I?
I'm part of a plant, too. I grow deep into the ground and help to hold that plant in place, even when a strong wind blows. What am I?	I'm what scientists use to look at a bacterium up close and personal. Just slide a one-celled organism at me! What am I?

©Macmillan/McGraw-Hill

Classifying Living Things

Fill in the blanks. 📖 Reading Skill: **Draw Conclusions** - questions 8, 20, 21

What Do Plants Have in Common?

1. Plant cells contain a green substance called _____.

2. Because of chlorophyll, green plants can use the _____ to make food.

3. All living things are made up of _____.

4. Plant cells have rigid _____ to support them.

5. Cells in plant stems, roots, and branches form tubes for transporting _____ and _____.

6. Groups of cells are organized into _____.

What Are the Major Plant Groups?

7. The science of finding patterns among living things is called _____.

8. Early systems for classifying plants were based on characteristics people could see easily, because _____.

9. Aristotle classified plants into three groups based on _____.

10. Scientists today divide plants into two large groups based on _____, not size or appearance.

11. Plants with tubelike tissues that carry food and water are classified as _____ plants.

12. The term "nonvascular" refers to plants _____.

What Are the Divisions of the Plant Kingdom?

13. Members of the plant kingdom all share common _____.

14. Scientists divided vascular plants into _____ and _____.

15. Scientists divide the plant kingdom into smaller groups, or _____.

What Makes Animals Different from Plants?

16. Two major factors that make animals different from plants are:

    a. _____, and

    b. _____.

17. The animal kingdom is divided into smaller groups called _____.

What Is a Fungus?

18. A fungus differs from green plants in that it does not make

    _____.

What Is a Protist?

19. The common characteristic of members of the protist kingdom is

    _____.

What Are Bacteria?

20. A microscopic organism consisting of one cell without a nucleus is a

    _____.

What Was "The Vine That Ate the South"?

21. Kudzu's nickname of "Foot-a-Night Vine" refers to

    _____.

©Macmillan/McGraw-Hill

Plant and Animal Cells

Diagrams like these show the different parts of something—in this case, plant cells and animal cells. In studying this type of diagram, the first step is to locate each feature or structure and read its label. When you have located a feature, remember what you have read about what it does. Notice its relationship to other features. If you have two diagrams side by side, look for similarities and differences between them.

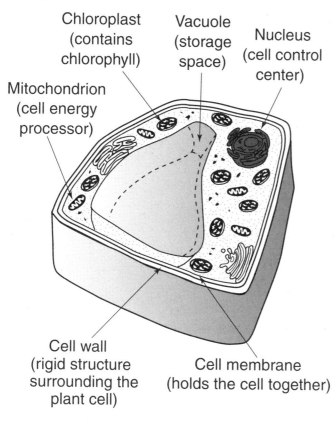

Chloroplast (contains chlorophyll)

Vacuole (storage space)

Nucleus (cell control center)

Mitochondrion (cell energy processor)

Cell wall (rigid structure surrounding the plant cell)

Cell membrane (holds the cell together)

Plant cell

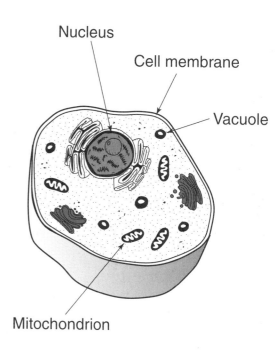

Nucleus

Cell membrane

Vacuole

Mitochondrion

Animal cell

Answer these questions about the diagram above.

1. What is the control center in plant cells called? _____

2. The large storage area inside a plant cell is called a(n) _____

3. What is the rigid structure surrounding a plant cell called?

_____

4. Does an animal cell have this structure? _____

5. What other feature does a plant cell have that an animal cell lacks?

_____

What Are the Major Plant Groups?

Charts like the one below are a way of organizing, or classifying information. They are like a visual outline—they start with the most general topic or group and break it down into smaller and smaller divisions. One clue to reading this kind of chart is the use of bold (dark) print. Bold print is used for the largest grouping in the chart: Plant Kingdom. Lighter letters are used to label smaller divisions.

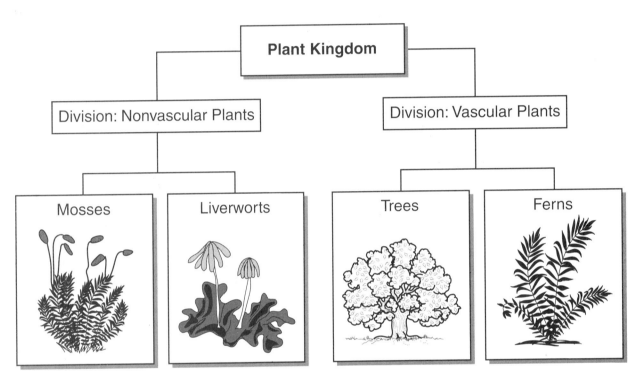

Answer these questions about the diagram above.

1. The plant kingdom is divided into two major groups. They are:

   _____

2. In which major group do trees belong? _____

3. In which major group do ferns belong? _____

4. From the chart, give one example of a nonvascular plant.

   _____

5. What is the only grouping in this chart that includes both trees and mosses?

   _____

Classifying Living Things

Fill in the blanks.

Vocabulary

cell walls
bacterium
protists
chlorophyll
vascular
classification
nonvascular
fungus

1. An organism that absorbs food from dead organisms and waste is called a(n) _____.

2. Plants that have tubelike structures up and down the stems are _____ plants.

3. Finding patterns among living things is called _____.

4. Algae and other tiny organisms that live in water are classified as _____.

5. The green chemical found in many plants is _____.

6. A moss is an example of a(n) _____ plant.

7. An organism of a single cell with no nucleus that could make you sick is a(n) _____.

8. Plant cells have rigid _____, which animal cells do not have.

Answer the following questions.

9. What do plants need to live and grow?

_____

_____

_____

10. Why was kudzu first considered a helpful plant? What happened to change people's minds about kudzu?

_____

_____

_____

© Macmillan/McGraw-Hill

Classifying Living Things

Vocabulary			
food	waste	many	flu-like
rise	cheeses	fungus	diseases

Fill in the blanks.

A fungus can't move around or make its own _____. Fungi

absorb food from decaying organisms and _____ in the

environment. A fungus can be one celled or _____ celled.

Some fungi contain chemicals that fight _____. Others

keep our environment clean. A fungus turns _____ sharp

and tangy. Yeast, another fungus, helps bread to _____.

Certain fungi produce problems. Athlete's foot, an itchy disease, is another

_____. Others that grow in damp places like basements cause

_____ symptoms.

Roots, Stems and Leaves

Fill in the blanks. Reading Skill: **Draw Conclusions** - questions 6, 18

How Do a Plant's Parts Help It Survive?

1. Foods such as beets and carrots are the _____ of different plants.

2. Roots help plants survive in three main ways:

   a. _____,

   b. _____, and

   c. _____.

3. A layer of tough cells that protect the growing tip of the root is called the _____.

4. A large thick root with a few hairy branching roots is a(n) _____.

5. Grasses and similar plants have thin, hairy _____.

6. Plants with fibrous roots thrive in dry regions because

   _____

7. _____, like those of a corn plant, grow like fingers out of the bottom of the stem.

8. Water and minerals pass through the root's _____ and move upward in the _____ to all the parts of the plant, while food flows downward in the _____.

How Are Stems Similar?

9. Plant stems support the _____ and _____.

10. The transportation system in plant stems has three basic parts: _____, _____, and _____.

11. Besides providing support and transportation, some plant stems are storage places for _____ and _____.

What Are Leaves?

12. The leaves of a maple tree, which hang singly, are _____ leaves.

13. Leaves that grow in clusters are _____ leaves.

14. The epidermis secretes a waxy coating called the _____, which keeps water inside the leaf.

15. The food-making structures inside leaf cells are _____.

16. Besides sunlight, chloroplasts need three things to make food: _____, _____, and _____.

17. Air comes through tiny pores in the bottom of the leaves called _____.

18. Different leaf shapes, such as these, have different purposes:
    a. broad, flat green surfaces: _____
    b. cactus spines: _____
    c. Venus's-flytrap leaves: _____

19. When water evaporates from the leaves, more water moves up through the plant to replace the lost water in a process called _____.

How Do Orchids Grow?

20. Some orchids in tropical forests have _____, which dangle high in the air.

How Do a Plant's Parts Help It Survive?

These cutaway diagrams show you the inner structures of a plant root. To understand diagrams like these, read each label and locate the feature or structure it names. If the label gives extra information about the structure, read that too. Notice that the second diagram, a cross-section of the root, is a close-up view of a part of the first drawing. See how it relates to the larger drawing of the root.

Parts of a Root

Xylem (ZIGH·luhm) Tissue through which water and minerals flow up through the plant

Cortex (KAWR·teks) A layer just inside the epidermis of roots and stems. It stores food.

Epidermis (ep·i·DUR·mis) The outermost layer of a root, stem, or leaf

Root cap A thin covering made up of cells. It protects the root tip as it grows into the soil.

Root hairs

Phloem (FLOH·em) Tissue through which food from the leaves moves down through a plant

Cambium (KAM·bee·um) The cambium is a layer that separates the xylem from the phloem. The cambium is where new xylem and phloem grow.

Water and minerals enter the root hairs. They pass through the root s cortex to the xylem. They then move up the xylem, into the plant s stem, and to all parts of the plant.

Answer these questions about the diagram above.

1. What root layer is next to the epidermis? _____

2. What protects the lower tip of a root? _____

3. Describe where the xylem and phloem are located in a root.

_____

4. What two structures do water and minerals pass through to get into the xylem?

_____

5. Which way does water move in the xylem—up or down? _____

What Are Leaves?

The drawings show the parts of leaves along with a cross-section diagram of a leaf's inner structure. To identify the parts of both types of leaves, read the label and follow the leader lines to the drawing. Notice how the same part looks slightly different in the two leaves. The cross-section diagram is the edge of a leaf, greatly magnified.

Parts of Leaves

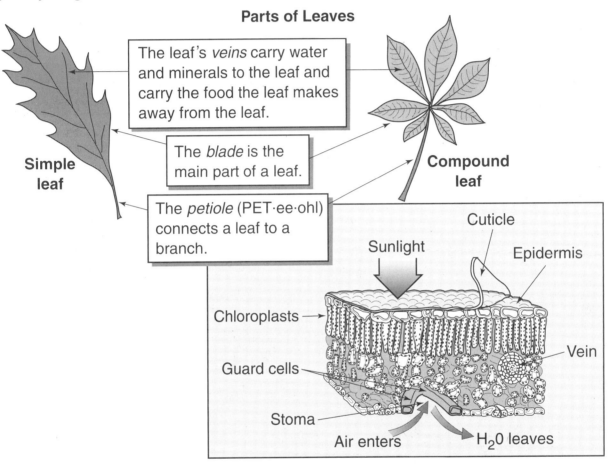

Simple leaf

The leaf's *veins* carry water and minerals to the leaf and carry the food the leaf makes away from the leaf.

The *blade* is the main part of a leaf.

The *petiole* (PET·ee·ohl) connects a leaf to a branch.

Compound leaf

Sunlight

Cuticle

Epidermis

Chloroplasts

Vein

Guard cells

Stoma

Air enters

H_2O leaves

Answer these questions about the diagram above.

1. Which type of leaf comes in clusters? _____

2. The structure that attaches a leaf to a branch is called a(n) _____.

3. What is the outermost cell layer in a leaf called? _____

4. What leaf structures can you see in both the cross section and the drawings?

_____

5. Besides water, the diagram shows two other things being supplied to the cells in the leaf. What are those things? _____

Roots, Stems, And Leaves

Fill in the blanks

1. Leaves that grow in clusters are called _____ leaves.

2. A layer of roots and stems that stores food is the _____

3. Water and minerals flow up from the roots through the _____.

4. The _____ is a layer in a root that separates the xylem from the phloem.

5. A _____ protects the root tip as it grows into the soil.

6. A leaf makes food in cells that contain _____.

7. The process of _____ occurs when water vapor evaporates from the leaves, and more water moves up through the plant to replace the lost water.

8. Food flows down through the _____ of the root.

9. The outermost layer of a root, stem, or leaf is called the _____.

Answer each question.

10. Describe the path water travels through a plant. What happens to the water?

_____

_____

_____

_____

11. Name two plants whose leaves we use for food, two plants whose stems we use for food, and two plants whose roots we use for food.

_____

_____

Roots, Stems, and Leaves

Vocabulary

secrete	minerals	food
chloroplasts	alive	water
carbon dioxide	cuticle	epidermis

Fill in the blanks.

The parts of a leaf work together to help keep the plant

_____. The outermost layer of a leaf is its

_____. Cells of the epidermis _____

a waxy coating, called a(n) _____. The cuticle helps

keep _____ from leaving the leaf. The leaf makes

_____ in cells between layers of the epidermis. These cells

contain _____, the green food factories of plants. In addition

to sunlight, these factories need water, _____, and the

_____ in air to make food.

The Importance of Plants

Fill in the blanks. 📖 Reading Skill: **Draw Conclusions** - questions 6, 10, 14

What Is Photosynthesis?

1. All living things need _____ to survive.

2. The energy that plants use in making food comes from _____.

3. The food-making process in plants is called _____.

4. Parts of plants are green because of a chemical called _____, located in the _____.

5. Inside the chloroplasts, _____ and _____ react chemically, helped by light energy.

6. Photosynthesis cannot occur without energy from _____.

7. Photosynthesis produces both _____ and _____.

8. Photosynthesis sets up a relationship between plants and animals:

    a. Plants give off _____, which animals breathe, into the air.

    b. Animals breathe out _____, which plants use in photo-synthesis.

9. Plants and animals break up sugar, releasing energy, in the process of _____.

How Do Leaves Change Color?

10. The yellow and orange colors in leaves aren't visible during the summer because leaves have too much _____.

11. When temperatures get colder, the green chlorophyll _____ and _____.

How Does Water Get from Roots to Leaves?

12. Plants are made up of about 70 to 95 percent _____.

13. Plants lose water through _____ from their leaves.

14. Water and minerals from the soil enter through the plant's

_____.

What Parts of Plants Do You Eat?

15. When you eat cabbage and spinach or drink tea, you are ingesting the _____ of plants.

16. When you eat ginger or potato, you are eating the _____ of plants.

17. Apples, oranges, and eggplant are the _____ of plants.

18. Peanuts, oats, and corn are all _____ of plants.

What Is Photosynthesis?

The leaf in this diagram is like a small factory where the process of photosynthesis takes place. The arrows in the diagram show the substances that enter and leave the leaves of green plants during this process. Notice the formula on top of the diagram that sums up the process. The arrow in the formula shows the results of the chemical processes that take place in the leaf.

Photosynthesis

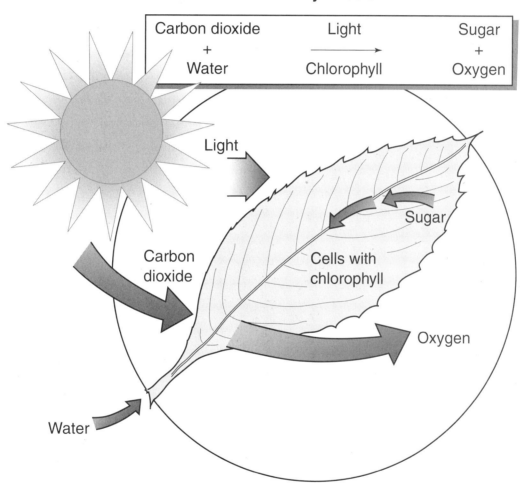

Answer these questions about the diagram above.

1. What is the source of the light used in photosynthesis? _____.

2. What chemical enters the leaf from the air? _____.

3. The chemical in the leaf cells is _____.

4. The leaf makes food in the form of _____.

5. What substance does the leaf give off into the air? _____.

Oxygen and Carbon Dioxide Exchange

When you see arrows in a diagram, you can expect that the diagram will show a process or cycle. The arrows indicate the direction of movement or change. This diagram shows the cycle by which plants and animals exchange oxygen and carbon dioxide. It involves two processes—photosynthesis and respiration. Follow the paths of the arrows in the diagram to track these substances as they transfer energy from plants to animals and back again.

Photosynthesis Hydrogen (from water) and carbon dioxide join in the presence of sunlight and chlorophyll to form sugars and oxygen.

The oxygen is released into the air.
- - - - - - - - - - - - - - - - -
The sugars that form are stored in green plants.

The water and carbon dioxide that form are released into the air.

Respiration In respiration, which occurs in plants and animals, sugars and oxygen join to produce water, carbon dioxide, and energy.

Answer these questions about the diagram above.

1. What two substances are produced by green plants during photosynthesis?

   _____.

2. Animals breathe in the _____ that is released into the air during photosynthesis.

3. During respiration, water, _____, and _____ are produced.

4. The process of _____ occurs in both plants and animals.

The Importance of Plants

Fill in the blanks.

1. Animals breathe out _____, which plants need to survive.

2. The process during which the cells break apart the sugar to make energy is called _____.

3. Water and dissolved minerals from the soil enter the plant through the plant's _____.

4. Plants are made up of 75–90 percent _____.

5. The Sun's energy is trapped and stored in the plant as _____.

6. Leaves are generally green because they contain _____.

7. When water evaporates from the leaves, it is called _____.

8. The food-making process of plants is called _____.

Answer the following questions.

9. What external factors make leaves change colors in the fall?

   _____

   _____

10. What happens during photosynthesis? What parts do carbon dioxide, water, light, chlorophyll, chloroplasts, sugar, and oxygen play in photosynthesis?

    _____

    _____

    _____

    _____

11. How does the process of photosynthesis help animals survive?

    _____

    _____

The Importance of Plants

Vocabulary

photosynthesis	orange	leaves
green	red	summer
temperature	evergreens	cloudy

Fill in the blanks.

In some areas, each autumn, _____ on all plants except

_____ change color. These yellow and _____

colors were inside the leaves ever since _____. However, the

colors weren't visible because of too much _____ chlorophyll

in the leaves. The chlorophyll, which is used in _____, slowly

breaks down and vanishes when the _____ begin to drop.

Where it's clear and cool you'll see another color— _____. In

warmer climates where the sky is _____, you wouldn't see

this color.

Plants and Their Parts

Circle the letter of the best answer.

1. The food-making process that uses sunlight is called
   - a. bacterium.
   - b. nonvascular.
   - c. photosynthesis.
   - d. transpiration.

2. What do plants NOT need to live and grow?
   - a. water
   - b. humans
   - c. minerals
   - d. carbon dioxide

3. The layer that separates the xylem and the phloem in a plant's stem is the
   - a. cambium.
   - b. cortex.
   - c. epidermis.
   - d. frond.

4. The release of energy from sugar is called
   - a. fertilization.
   - b. photosynthesis.
   - c. respiration.
   - d. transpiration.

5. A plant that has tubelike structures up and down the stem is a(n)
   - a. fungus.
   - b. protist.
   - c. bacteria.
   - d. vascular plant.

6. The green food factories of plants are called
   - a. stomata.
   - b. petioles.
   - c. chloroplasts.
   - d. veins.

7. Some parts of plants have an outer layer called the
   - a. cambium.
   - b. epidermis.
   - c. phloem.
   - d. xylem.

8. Growing roots are protected by a(n)
   - a. cortex.
   - b. epidermis.
   - c. rhizome.
   - d. root cap.

© Macmillan/McGraw-Hill

Circle the letter of the best answer.

9. Almost 99% of water that enters a plant's roots is given off by

   a. fertilization.   **b.** reproduction.

   c. respiration.   **d.** transpiration.

10. Most transpiration occurs in the

   a. xylem.   **b.** leaves.

   c. roots.   **d.** stem.

11. The substance that uses the Sun's energy to make food for plants is

   a. chlorophyll.   **b.** minerals.

   c. spores.   **d.** water.

12. A leaf's cuticle

   a. is responsible for reproduction.

   b. helps keep water in the leaf.

   c. should be cut every year.

   d. separates the xylem from the phloem.

13. Plants that have tissue through which food and water move are said to be

   a. bacteria.   **b.** nonvascular.

   c. protist.   **d.** vascular.

14. Energy is stored in plants as

   a. sugars.   **b.** carbon dioxide.

   c. chlorophyll.   **d.** water.

Chapter Summary

1. What is the name of the chapter you just finished reading?

   _____

   _____

2. What are four vocabulary words you learned in the chapter?
   Write a definition for each.

   _____

   _____

   _____

   _____

   _____

   _____

   _____

3. What are two main ideas that you learned in this chapter?

   _____

   _____

   _____

   _____

   _____

Plant Diversity

A Venn diagram is a good way to compare and contrast two things, such as how plants reproduce and how they respond. In the part of each circle that does not overlap the other, write the things that make each item different from the other. Where the circles overlap, write the things that the items have in common. Look at the example below.

Example

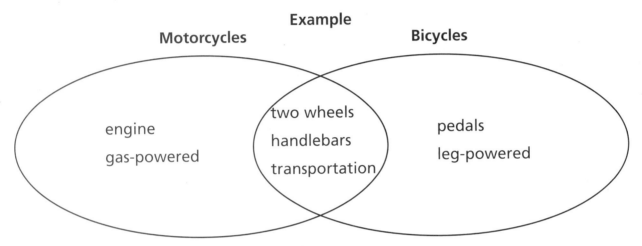

Motorcycles

engine
gas-powered

two wheels
handlebars
transportation

Bicycles

pedals
leg-powered

Compare and contrast angiosperms and gymnosperms by filling in the Venn diagram below. Use the words in the word bank.

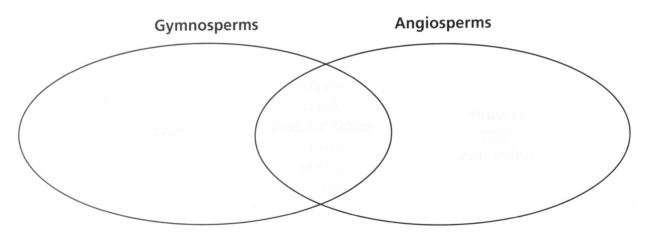

Gymnosperms

Angiosperms

Word Bank		
cones	cotyledon	flowers
fruit	leaves	pollen
roots	seeds	stem
vascular tissue		

©Macmillan/McGraw-Hill

Compare and Contrast

What's the difference between **comparing** and **contrasting**? To compare things, we point out how they're alike. To contrast things, we point out how they're different.

Two things may be almost exactly alike, but not quite. Even identical twins aren't identical in all ways. One twin may smile differently or have a happier personality than the other. One may be very shy, while the other is just the opposite!

Think about each set of things below. Then write at least one way the things are alike and one way they're different.

	Alike	Different
1. A frog and a butterfly		
2. A fern and a moss		
3. A belt and suspenders		
4. A cassette tape and a CD		
5. A plane, a train, and a bicycle		
6. A book, a magazine, and a newspaper		
7. An actor, a dancer, and a painter		

©Macmillan/McGraw-Hill

Alike and Different

As you read books and articles, you may find that an author compares and contrasts people or things. To help you remember the story, make a chart on which you can compare and contrast the people or things yourself.

Read the following story, then use the chart to compare and contrast the characters. Add more features from the story to the chart.

Maria, Martina, and Mario are 12-year-old triplets. The two girls have dark hair. Their brother, Mario, is blond. They all have blue eyes.

Maria and Mario are very good singers. Martina plays piano for them. Mario also plays a mean guitar. The triplets want to start a band, but they can't seem to find the time. Mario and Martina are on the soccer team. They have practice every day after school and games on Saturdays! Maria takes dance three days a week. She often has shows or recitals on Sunday afternoons!

The kids finally had a chance to play and sing as a band. they asked a friend to play drums with them. The band performed at a celebration when Martina and Mario's soccer team won the regional championship! Maria even danced the macarena and got all the parents and guests to join in!

	Maria	Martina	Mario
Is a girl			
Is a boy			
Has dark hair			
Is blond			
Sings well			

©Macmillan/McGraw-Hill

Plants Without Seeds

Fill in the blanks. Reading Skill: **Compare and Contrast** - questions 5, 6, 7, 11, 17, 20, 21, 22, 23

How Do Mosses Get Water?

1. Plants without tubelike structures to carry water are called _____.

2. Two types of nonvascular plants are _____ and _____.

3. Mosses are anchored in place by hairlike fibers called _____, which take the place of _____.

4. Rhizoids, like other parts of mosses and liverworts, can take in water from their _____.

5. While most common plants grow from seeds, mosses and liverworts grow from cells called _____.

6. Ferns and club mosses are vascular plants, but they are like mosses because they use spores to _____.

7. Because vascular tissue is made of long, tubelike cells, _____ plants can grow taller and thicker than mosses.

What Are Ferns?

8. The leaves, or fronds, of a fern grow from a(n) _____, which is an underground stem.

9. The bottom sides of some fronds are covered with _____.

10. Spores are spread around the fern when the spore cases _____.

How Do the Life Cycles of Mosses and Ferns Differ?

11. Mosses and ferns both use _____ to reproduce.

12. A plant that reproduces with one type of cell is reproducing by _____ reproduction.

13. Moss spores grow into moss plants with both _____ and _____ branches.

14. Male branches produce _____, while female branches produce _____.

15. In sexual reproduction, a male sex cell _____ the egg, which grows into a stalk topped with a spore case.

16. Spores that are released onto damp ground grow into new _____.

17. Both mosses and ferns alternate sexual and asexual reproduction, a process called _____.

18. Fern spores grow into heart-shaped plants that produce _____ and _____ sex cells.

19. If male and female cells from the plant join, the fertilized egg grows into a(n) _____.

What Were the Ancestors of Plants?

20. To find the ancestors of plants, scientists first looked at other organisms that carry on _____.

21. Green algae are like plants in various ways, including having strong _____ containing cellulose.

22. Green algae and plants store food as _____.

23. Scientists concluded that the first land plants to develop from algae were probably nonvascular plants similar to _____.

Moss Life Cycle

The arrows indicate the direction of movement or the different stages in a process. This diagram illustrates the life cycle of mosses. Because it is a cycle—a repeating process—it does not have a beginning or an end but moves in a circle. Follow the arrows to trace the stages in this cycle.

Life Cycle of a Moss

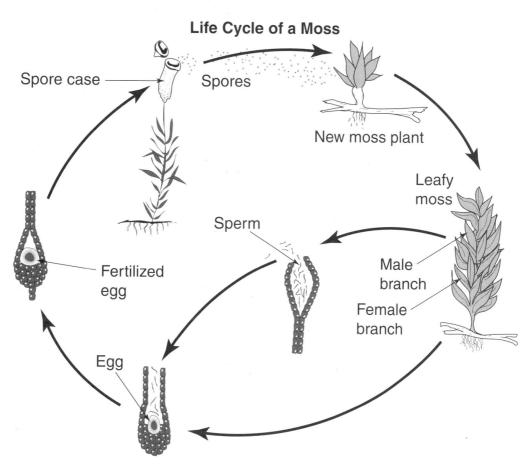

Spore case — Spores — New moss plant — Leafy moss — Male branch — Female branch — Sperm — Fertilized egg — Egg

Answer these questions about the diagram above.

1. The two arrows leading from the leafy moss plant show that it produces two kinds of cells.

   a. _____ and

   b. _____ cells.

2. What happens when the sperm joins the egg? _____

3. What grows from the fertilized egg? _____

4. New moss plants begin to grow when _____ are released.

Fern Life Cycle

In a diagram of a process or cycle, arrows are used to show the different stages in that process. This diagram shows the stages in the life cycle of a fern—how it grows and produces new fern plants. By following the arrows in the diagram, you can follow that cycle.

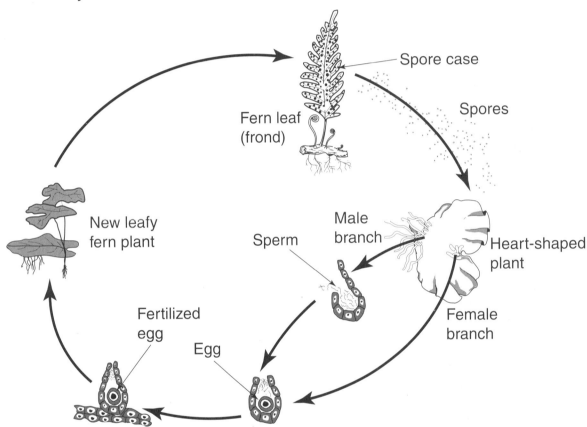

Answer these questions about the diagram above.

1. Where are the spore cases of a fern located?

_____

2. After fern spores are released, what is the next stage in the cycle?

_____

3. When a sperm cell and an egg cell join, the next stage in the cycle is a(n)

_____

4. Does a new leafy fern plant grow from spores or from a fertilized egg?

_____

Plants Without Seeds

Fill in the blanks.

1. The hairlike fibers that hold mosses to the ground are called _____.

2. The stage when a plant needs both male and female sex cells in order to reproduce is called _____ reproduction.

3. Fronds grow above the ground from an underground stem called a(n) _____.

4. The production of spores is a form of _____ reproduction.

5. The first land plants to develop from algae were similar to _____.

6. Ferns are _____ plants.

7. Mosses grow from special cells called _____.

8. The leaves of a fern are called _____.

9. When a male sex cell and a female sex cell join together, _____ takes place.

Answer the following questions.

10. Explain the alternation of generations.

_____

_____

_____

11. How are mosses and ferns alike? How are they different?

_____

_____

_____

Plants Without Seeds

Vocabulary

liverworts	pillows	vascular
trees	spores	cells
centimeters	rhizoids	seedless

Fill in the blanks.

Neither mosses nor their close relatives the _____, have

roots. Hairlike fibers called _____ anchor these plants in

place. Both cling to sheltered rocks, moist soil, and the shady side of

_____. Mosses and liverworts are nonvascular, without the

long tubelike structures that _____ plants have. These are

tiny plants, only 2 to 5 _____ high. Mosses' leaves grow only

one or two _____ thick. Mosses resemble green, fuzzy

_____. Liverworts look like flat leaves. Both are

_____ plants, growing from _____.

Plants with Seeds

Fill in the blanks.. Reading Skill: **Compare and Contrast** - questions 2, 7, 8, 9, 10, 13, 15

How Do Seed Plants Differ?

1. The seeds of plants contain a(n) _____ and _____ .

2. Seed plants that produce flowers are _____, while those that do not flower are _____ .

3. Evergreen trees, such as pines and firs, are _____ .

4. Gymnosperms first appeared on Earth about _____ years ago.

5. Most fruits, nuts, and vegetables we eat come from _____ .

6. The four divisions of gymnosperms are _____, _____, _____, and _____ .

7. Gymnosperms are alike in producing their seeds on the _____ of female cones.

8. The leaves of most gymnosperms are shaped like _____ .

9. While most gymnosperms are evergreen, the larch is _____ and loses its leaves each fall.

10. Conifer _____ lose less water than the wider leaves of flowering plants.

What Are Angiosperms?

11. Angiosperms are the largest division in the plant kingdom, with about _____ different members.

12. The smallest angiosperm is a flowering plant that floats on the water called _____.

13. Gymnosperms live mainly in cold, dry, northern climates, but _____ live in all climates and all parts of the world.

14. Angiosperms that live off other plants are _____.

15. Two ways to distinguish an angiosperm from a gymnosperm are:

    a. _____, and

    b. _____.

What Are Cotyledons?

16. The two classes of angiosperms are based on the number of _____, leaflike structures inside a seed, they have.

17. Besides having one cotyledon, _____ have parallel leaf veins.

18. Maple trees and roses are dicots, which have _____ cotyledons.

Why Do Flowers Have Aromas?

19. The main purpose of a flower's aroma is _____.

20. Inside a flower, insects pick up grains of _____, which contain _____.

21. When the insect travels to another flower, it transfers pollen to _____, helping the plant reproduce.

© Macmillan/McGraw-Hill

What Are Cotyledons?

A chart like the one below organizes information to show similarities and differences. To read a chart, start with the title. It tells you what the overall subject is.
Then read the headings for each column or section. In this chart, for example, the
first column, headed "Characteristics," lists four characteristics of seed plants. The
next two columns compare those characteristics in monocots and dicots, the two
classes of angiosperms.

Characteristics of Monocots and Dicots		
Characteristics	**Monocots**	**Dicots**
Cotyledons	One	Two
Leaf veins	Parallel	Branched
Flower parts	Multiples of three	Multiples of four or five
Vascular system	Scattered in bundles	In rings

Answer these questions about the diagram above.

1. Which class of plant—monocot or dicot—has two cotyledons?

    _____

2. The leaf veins of a dicot are _____.

3. The flower parts of a monocot occur in multiples of _____.

4. In the stem of a _____, the vascular system is scattered in bundles.

Insects Help Plants Reproduce

The pictures below show how insects pollinate jack-in-the-pulpit flowers. Pollen sticks to the insect. The insect gets trapped in the flower by its smooth sides. As the insect moves around inside the flower, it pollinates the flower, and begins the reproduction of a new plant.

The awful-smelling jack-in-the-pulpit flower attracts insects that help the plant reproduce.

Answer the following questions about the picture above.

1. What does the insect fly into?

   _____

   _____

2. What does the pollen stick to?

   _____

   _____

3. What causes the insect to move around inside the flower and pollinate it?

   _____

   _____

© Macmillan/McGraw-Hill

Plants with Seeds

Fill in the blanks.

1. Angiosperms whose seeds contain two cotyledons are called _____ for short.

2. A(n) _____ contains an undeveloped plant and stored food.

3. The aroma of a plant serves to attract _____.

4. The division of gymnosperms that include the deciduous plants is the _____.

5. Seed plants that produce flowers are called _____.

6. Plants whose seeds contain only one cotyledon are called _____ for short.

7. Seed plants that do not produce flowers are called _____.

8. A tiny leaflike structure inside a seed is a(n) _____.

Answer each question.

9. What characteristics could you use to help you decide if a plant was a monocot or a dicot?

_____

_____

_____

_____

_____

10. What characteristics could you use to help you decide if a plant was a gymnosperm or an angiosperm?

_____

_____

Vocabulary

seed
cotyledon
gymnosperms
dicots
angiosperms
insect
conifer
parasite
monocots

Plants with Seeds

Vocabulary

evergreens	conifers	female
leaves	flowers	Gymnosperms
deciduous	cuticle	seed

Fill in the blanks.

_____ first appeared when most of Earth was cold and dry, about 250 million years ago. Unlike angiosperms, gymnosperms do not produce _____. Gymnosperms reproduce from seeds found on the scales of _____ cones. Concealed within each _____ is an undeveloped plant and stored food. The _____ of gymnosperms are needle-like and are constantly being replaced. Most gymnosperms are _____. Some conifers are called _____ meaning they lose leaves each fall. The needles of _____ have a small surface area and are covered with a thick _____.

Name_____ Date_____

Flowers and Seeds

Fill in the blanks. 📖 Reading Skill: **Compare and Contrast** - questions 4, 6, 9, 17

How Do Flowers Differ?

1. A flower that has sepals, petals, stamens, and pistils is termed a(n) _____.

2. A flower containing both male and female parts is called a(n) _____.

3. A "female" flower has pistils, but no _____ and would be called a(n) _____ flower.

4. A single oak tree has both _____ and _____ flowers, but a willow tree has either male flowers or female flowers.

5. Holly berries are the _____ of a holly tree with female flowers.

What Are Pollination and Fertilization?

6. Both large and tiny seeds _____ in the same way.

7. Pollen on a flower's _____ contains male sex cells.

8. The transfer of pollen from anther to stigma is called _____.

9. The transfer of pollen within the same flower is called _____, while carrying the pollen to another flower is called _____.

10. A pollen grain forms a tube leading to the flower's _____, where sperm _____ an egg cell.

11. A fertilized egg cell develops into a(n) _____.

What Is in a Seed?

12. The three main parts of a seed are:

    a. an immature plant, or the _____,

    b. a tough covering, or the _____, and

    c. the _____, where food is stored as starch.

© Macmillan/McGraw-Hill

13. The two steps in growing a new plant from a seed are

_____ and _____, or sprouting.

14. To grow, seeds often must move far away to avoid _____ from other plants.

15. Animals that eat ripe _____ help spread seeds through their

_____.

16. Wind and animals also move the cones and seeds of _____, which do not have fruit.

What Is the Life Cycle of a Conifer?

17. Since _____ don't produce flowers or fruits, their life cycle is not the same as angiosperms.

18. A pine tree produces both _____ and _____ cones.

19. Pollen from a male cone is carried by wind to a female cone, where it

_____ an egg cell.

Ways Plants Are Pollinated

These diagrams show two ways in which plants are pollinated. To compare the two methods, first read the explanations under the drawings. Then read the labels on the drawings and follow the leader lines to identify each part of a flower. Notice that the flowers have similar parts.

Pollination

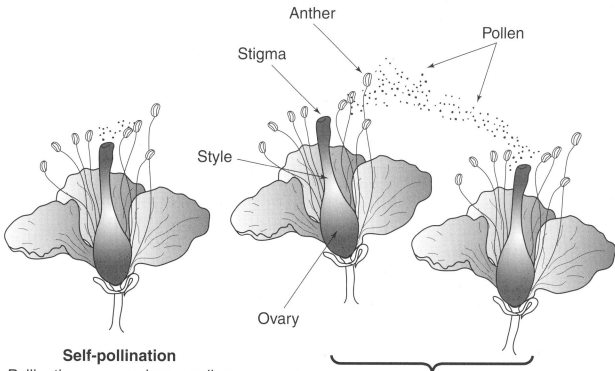

Self-pollination
Pollination occurs when a pollen grain from an anther reaches the stigma. This flower is pollinating itself because its own pollen is reaching its own stigma.

Cross-pollination
Pollination can occur between two or more flowers on separate plants. Here the pollen of one flower reaches the stigma of another.

Answer these questions about the diagram above.

1. Grains of pollen come from the _____ of a flower.

2. The top of the flower's style is called the _____.

3. Which method of pollination requires at least two flowers?

   _____.

4. In both types of pollination, pollen is transferred to the _____ of a flower.

Process of Fertilization

These flower diagrams show the process of fertilization that takes place after pollination. Notice that each step in the process is numbered. Read the labels on the diagrams to identify each part of a flower. As you read each step, check the diagram and locate the parts that are mentioned.

Fertilization

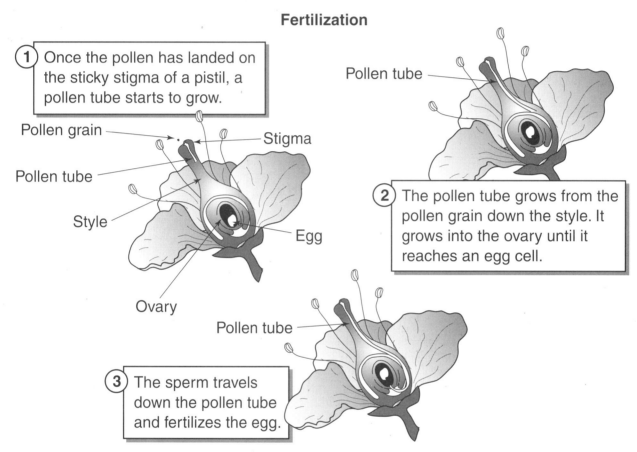

① Once the pollen has landed on the sticky stigma of a pistil, a pollen tube starts to grow.

Pollen grain
Stigma
Pollen tube
Style
Egg
Ovary

Pollen tube

② The pollen tube grows from the pollen grain down the style. It grows into the ovary until it reaches an egg cell.

Pollen tube

③ The sperm travels down the pollen tube and fertilizes the egg.

Answer these questions about the diagram above.

1. Where do pollen grains land to cause the pollen tube to grow?

   _____

2. Where are the egg cells of a flower located? _____

3. The new structure that grows from a pollen grain is called the

   _____

4. How does sperm reach and fertilize the egg?

   _____

© Macmillan/McGraw-Hill

Flowers and Seeds

Fill in the blanks.

Vocabulary

fruit

pistil

pollination

ovary

embryo

seed coat

anther

wind

1. The transfer of pollen from the anther to the stigma is called _____.

2. A(n) _____ is an immature plant inside a seed.

3. A mature ripened ovary of a plant is called the _____.

4. Many seeds are scattered by the _____.

5. Grains of pollen are found in the _____ of a flower.

6. The base of the pistil is the _____.

7. The ovary in a flower is found at the base of the _____.

8. The outer covering of a seed is called a(n) _____.

Answer the following questions.

9. Describe the life cycle of a conifer.

_____

_____

_____

_____

10. What is the difference between self-pollination and cross-pollination?

_____

_____

_____

_____

Flowers and Seeds

Vocabulary

dispersal	competition	warm	germination
wastes	ovary	wind	

Fill in the blanks.

Before seeds produce plants, they move to where they can sprout. This is

known as seed _____. Seeds travel far from the parent plant

to avoid _____ for sunlight and water. Some seeds have para-

chutes that are blown by the _____. Others are transported

by animals that eat the plant's ripened _____, which is called

a fruit. Animals deposit the seeds in their _____. For sprout-

ing, which is called _____, seeds need water and a(n)

_____ temperature.

Plant Responses and Adaptations

Fill in the blanks. Reading Skill: **Compare and Contrast** - questions 6, 12, 14

What Are Tropisms?

1. Light, heat, and other things that produce a response are examples of a(n) _____.

2. A plant's movement toward or away from a stimulus is called _____.

3. Plant roots grow downward in response to _____.

4. The response of a plant to changes in light is called _____.

5. The roots of a willow tree show _____ as they grow toward a water source.

6. In Darwin's experiment, the plant shoots with _____ turned toward light, while the plants without tips did not.

7. Scientist Fritz Went believed that a(n) _____ allowed the plant shoots to bend toward light.

8. Chemicals that stimulate plant growth are called _____.

9. Plant shoots bend toward light because auxins cause cell growth on the _____ of the stem, making it longer.

How Do Plants Survive?

10. Adaptations help plants survive in many kinds of _____.

11. A desert plant such as a cactus has adaptations for _____, _____, and _____.

12. "Long-day" plants such as spinach bloom at a time of year when there is more _____ than _____.

Why Do Plants Compete?

13. Plants compete with each other for _____,
    _____, and _____.

14. Trees in a forest have more leaves at the top in order to get
    more _____.

How Do Plants Use Chemicals to Survive?

15. Plants such as creosote produce _____ that harm other plants.

16. Other plants make chemicals that discourage _____
    and _____ from feeding on or infecting them.

What Are Tropisms?

These drawings illustrate a famous experiment in the history of science. It proved something about plant tropisms—the processes that make parts of a plant tend to turn or move in a certain direction. Darwin's experiment, pictured here, used two plant shoots to show one kind of plant tropism. Study the drawings to see what that process is.

Darwin's Experiment

Plant tip

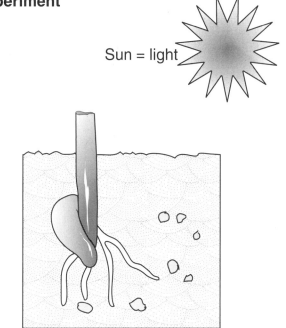

Sun = light

Answer these questions about the diagram above.

1. How is the plant shoot on the right different from the one on the left?

   _____

2. Is the plant on the right bending or growing straight up?

   _____

3. What part of the plant on the left is bending? _____

4. Toward what is the plant bending?

   _____

5. In your own words, summarize what this experiment showed.

   _____

   _____

How Do Plants Survive?

The picture below shows the difference between short-day and long-day plants. In the diagram, the shaded part of the clock shows night.

SHORT DAY, LONG-DAY PLANTS

Light

PLANT A
Leaves,
no flowers

PLANT B
Leaves
and flowers

Light

Leaves
and flowers

Leaves,
no flowers

Answer the following questions about the picture above.

1. Which plant has flowers and leaves when there is more daylight than nighttime?

   _____

2. Which plant has leaves and no flowers when there is more nighttime than daylight?

   _____

3. Which plant's flowers would bloom during the mid-summer months?

   _____

4. Which plant's flowers would bloom during the fall months?

   _____

Plant Responses and Adaptations

Vocabulary

gravitropism

short-day

stimulus

adaptation

long-day

hydrotropism

response

tropism

Fill in the blanks.

1. Anything in the environment that produces a response is called a(n) _____.

2. If a plant bends toward a stimulus, its change is called a positive _____.

3. A plant that grows toward the pull of gravity shows _____.

4. Some plants, such as squash and grape plants, show a _____ to touch.

5. A(n) _____ helps an organism survive in its environment.

6. Plants that bloom when there is more darkness and less daylight are called _____ plants.

7. Plants whose roots grow toward a source of water are showing _____.

8. Plants that bloom when there is much more daylight than darkness are called _____ plants.

Answer each question.

9. What is an adaptation? Give an example.

_____

_____

_____

10. What are four strategies plants use to win the battle for sunlight, nutrients, and water?

_____

_____

_____

© Macmillan/McGraw-Hill

Plant Responses and Adaptations

Vocabulary

storing	water	adapted
response	deserts	adaptations
night–time	center	
bloom	insects	

Fill in the blanks.

The reason plants survive in rain forests, the arctic, and _____

is because they have _____ to their environments. Desert

plants have _____ for collecting, _____ and

saving water. Cactus plants have a thick, waxy coating to help prevent

_____ loss. This plant's stomata open at

_____, when it's cooler. Moisture is stored in the

_____ of the cactus plant. Carnivorous plants obtain some

nutrients by trapping and digesting _____. When there is

more daylight than darkness, long-day plants _____. This

flowering _____is known as photoperodism.

©Macmillan/McGraw-Hill

Plant Diversity

Circle the letter of the best answer.

1. Something that causes a living thing to react is a(n)
   - a. anther.
   - b. dicot.
   - c. earned behavior.
   - d. stimulus.

2. When a plant slowly bends toward or away from a stimulus it is called a
   - a. conifer.
   - b. embryo.
   - c. gravity.
   - d. tropism.

3. Plants that produce flowers are
   - a. angiosperms.
   - b. conifers.
   - c. gymnosperms.
   - d. tropisms.

4. Monocots contain only one
   - a. conifer.
   - b. cotyledon.
   - c. gymnosperms.
   - d. response.

5. A fruit is a seed's mature ripened
   - a. anther.
   - b. gymnosperm.
   - c. ovary.
   - d. stigma.

6. Most gymnosperms are
   - a. angiosperms.
   - b. evergreens.
   - c. deciduous.
   - d. violets.

7. The transfer of pollen from a flower's anther to its stigma is
   - a. adoption.
   - b. asexual reproduction.
   - c. pollination.
   - d. respiration.

© Macmillan/McGraw-Hill

Circle the letter of the best answer.

8. A flower's aroma attracts insects who carry
   a. food.   b. pollen.
   c. seeds.   d. water.

9. A flowering plant's response to the length of daylight is called
   a. hydrotropism.   b. mimicry.
   c. photoperiodism.   d. phototropism.

10. Conifers that lose their leaves in the fall are
    a. evergreens.   b. deciduous.
    c. saplings.   d. young.

11. A desert plant collecting, storing, and saving water is an example of a(n)
    a. adaptation.
    b. reproduction.
    c. competition.
    d. stimulus.

12. What a plant or animal does after receiving a stimulus is an example of a(n)
    a. adaptation.   b. answer.
    c. response.   d. sexual reproduction.

13. A plant shows phototropism if it grows
    a. away from water.   b. down.
    c. towards light.   d. toward water.

©Macmillan/McGraw-Hill

Name_____ Date_____

Chapter Summary

1. What is the name of the chapter you just finished reading?

_____

_____

2. What are four vocabulary words you learned in the chapter?
Write a definition for each.

_____

_____

_____

_____

_____

_____

_____

_____

3. What are two main ideas that you learned in this chapter?

_____

_____

_____

_____

_____

_____

©Macmillan/McGraw-Hill

Animal Diversity

A graphic organizer like the one shown below can help you summarize a paragraph. Choose a paragraph from your textbook. Fill in the details for your paragraph under the heading marked "Details." Then, write your summary under the heading marked "Summary". You can see if your summary is correct by checking it against the details that you listed. Each detail should support your summary.

Details
1.
2.
3.
4.
5.
6.
7.
8.

Summary

©Macmillan/McGraw-Hill

Summarize

A summary should reflect the main idea of a paragraph and be supported by each of the details in the paragraph. Read the following paragraph entitled "Blending In." Underline each of the details in the paragraph. Then write a summary in the space provided.

Blending In

About 150 years ago, England was home to two kinds of peppered moths. One kind was light colored. The other kind was dark colored. Birds fed on both kinds of moths, many of which clung to the trunks of trees. However, gradually the light-colored moths seemed to be disappearing. The birds were eating more of these moths than the dark-colored ones. This happened because nearby factories were pouring dark, sticky smoke into the air. The smoke stuck to the trunks of trees. The light-colored moths stood out against this background. The dark-colored moths blended in with the background. Since the birds could more easily see the light-colored moths, the birds were eating more light-colored moths than dark-colored moths. This is an example of a kind of camouflage called protective coloration. The color of the dark peppered moths protected them from predators.

Summary

More Summarizing Paragraphs

A summary should also be short and easy to understand. Read the following paragraph entitled "Cells, Tissues, Organs, and Systems." Then choose the summary from the ones listed below that best reflects the paragraph.

Cells, Tissues, Organs, and Systems

The building blocks of living things are cells. Whether an animal grows hair or feathers depends on the kinds of cells it has. Scientists often study the cells of animals in order to best group them. Similar cells that have the same job or function come together to make a tissue. Tissues of different kinds come together to make an organ, like a heart or brain. Finally, a group of organs that work together to do a certain job make up an organ system. For example, an animal's digestive system includes its mouth, stomach, and intestines.

Summary

1. The building blocks of living things are cells.

2. Scientists often study the cells, tissues, and organs of animals in order to best group them.

3. Cells, the building blocks of all living things, form tissues; tissues come together to make organs; organs come together to make organ systems.

4. A heart is an organ.

©Macmillan/McGraw-Hill

Animal Structure and Function

Fill in the blanks. Reading Skill: **Summarize** - questions 6, 7

What Traits Are Used to Classify Animals?

1. The building blocks of all living things are _____.

2. Scientists study the cells of animals in order to best group or _____ them.

3. Similar cells that have the same job or function come together to make a(n) _____.

4. Tissues of different kinds come together to make a(n) _____, like a heart or brain.

5. An organ _____ is a group of organs that work together to do a certain job.

6. Animals that have backbones are members of a group called _____.

7. Members of the group of animals called _____ have no backbones.

8. One of the simplest kinds of animals is a sponge which belongs to a group called _____.

9. Hydra, anemones, and jellyfish belong to a group called _____ and do not have heads or tails.

10. _____, or flatworms, have flat bodies but no true organ systems.

11. Segmented worms or _____ have specialized organs such as jaws or gills as well as a circulatory, digestive, and nervous system.

12. The _____ group, or mollusks, include snails, clams, and octopuses and have a shell which may be either inside or outside of the mollusk's body.

13. Members of the largest animal group, _____, have tough outer skeletons, jointed legs, and a body made up of two, three, or more sections.

14. Unlike the arthropods, the _____ or echinoderms, have a skeleton inside their bodies.

15. Sharks and rays, which are part of the _____ group, have cartilage running down their backs in a chain of smaller parts.

16. Frogs, toads, and salamanders are _____ that live in water during the early stages of life.

17. The _____, the first group of vertebrates to grow and develop out of the water, breathe through their lungs and have waterpoof scales on their skins.

18. Members of the _____ group have feathers, wings, and strong but lightweight bones.

What Traits Are Used to Classify Animals?

The picture below shows the forelimbs of a bat, a cat, and an eagle. Even though the bat flies like the eagle, which is a type of bird, its forelimb more closely resembles the forelimb of the cat, a mammal.

Answer the following questions about the picture above.

1. Which two forelimbs look most like each other?

_____

_____

2. How do the bat's and the eagle's forelimbs differ?

_____

_____

3. How does the covering of the bat's and eagle's forelimbs differ?

_____

_____

Animal Structure and Function

There are five basic categories of vertebrates: fish, amphibians, reptiles, birds, and mammals. Due to adaptation to environment, the structure of vertebrates varies widely. The pictures show examples of each of these types of animals.

Answer the following questions about the picture above.

1. What are the main ways that fish differ from the other types of vertebrates?

_____

_____

2. How do the coverings of amphibians and reptiles differ?

_____

_____

3. How does the covering of the mammals differ from the other types of verte-brates?

_____

_____

©Macmillan/McGraw-Hill

Animal Structure and Function

Fill in the blanks.

Vocabulary

Agnatha

vertebrates

tissue

system

cells

invertebrates

Osteichthys

organ

1. Animals that have backbones are called _____.

2. Tissues of different kinds come together to make an _____.

3. _____ have a tough nerve cord that runs down the back instead of a backbone.

4. The building blocks of living things are _____.

5. An organ _____ is a group of organs that work together to do a certain job.

6. Animals that do not have backbones are called _____.

7. Similar cells that have the same job or function come together to make a _____.

8. _____, or bony fish, have bones instead of cartilage and a movable flap over their gills that helps them to breathe while staying still.

Answer each question.

9. What is the major difference between vertebrates and invertebrates?

_____

_____

10. How do cells come together to make organ systems?

_____

_____

11. What structure does bony fish, or Osteichthys, have that sharks do not have? How does this structure help bony fish to function?

_____

_____

_____

Animal Structure and Function

Vocabulary

system	invertebrates	organ
tissue	traits	cells
vertebrates	group	classify

Fill in the blanks.

The building blocks of living things are _____. Scientists study the cells of animals in order to best _____ them. Similar cells that have the same job or function come together to make a _____. Tissues of different kinds come together to make an _____, like a heart or brain. A group of organs that work together to do a certain job make up an organ _____. By studying cells, tissues, organs, and systems, scientists can _____ animals. Animals are divided into two large groups. One group, called _____, has backbones. The members of the other group have no backbones and are called _____. Vertebrates and invertebrates can be divided by _____ into smaller groups.

Animal Adaptations

Fill in the blanks. Reading Skill: **Summarize** - questions 5, 7, 8, 12, 15, 16, 18

How Do Animals Adapt?

1. An important group of adaptations helps an animal keep from getting eaten by a(n) _____.

2. In nature, looking like something else, especially something unpleasant, is called _____.

3. Monarch _____ (caterpillars) are protected from predators because they feed on milkweed which contains a substance that can make many animals ill.

4. _____ look like thorns, so predators stay away from them.

What Is Camouflage?

5. An animal that does not move, or moves very, very slowly and looks like its surroundings is using _____ to protect itself.

6. The wings of a leaf _____ are shaped like the leaves of a plant which makes it very hard to see.

7. Dark-colored moths that blend in with the background is an example of _____.

What Is Inherited?

8. A(n) _____ behavior is one that is not learned and is passed down from one generation to the next.

9. Inherited behavior, which is done automatically, is called _____.

10. The passing of inherited traits from parents to offspring is called _____.

11. Some traits are affected by both heredity and the _____.

What Is a Hybrid?

12. Living things that have parents that are quite different from each other, such as donkeys and horses, are called _____.

13. People sometimes _____ hybrids on purpose, since a hybrid may have more desirable traits than either of its parents.

14. Some people mate living things that are closely related in a process called _____.

15. A _____ is a product of the mating of individuals from two distinct breeds or varieties of the same species.

Why Is Diversity Important?

16. Animal _____ refers to a group of the same kind of animal in which there are lots of animals with different traits.

17. When an environment changes, only those animals that can _____ to the change will survive.

18. If the population is made up of animals with the same traits, and those traits do not help the animals survive in a changing environment, the whole _____ may die out.

©Macmillan/McGraw-Hill

How Do Animals Adapt?

The picture below shows two similar-looking insects. One is a yellow jacket which has a poison stinger. The other is a harmless fly called a syrphid. The syrphid is using an adaptation called mimicry to protect itself from predetors.

Answer the following questions about the picture above.

1. How do the yellow jacket and the syrphid look similar?

   _____

   _____

2. How do the yellow jacket and the syrphid look different?

   _____

   _____

3. How does looking like a yellow jacket help the syrphid protect itself from pre-detors?

   _____

   _____

What Is Camouflage?

The pictures below show two kinds of peppered moths against a dark tree. The darker peppered moth is harder for predators to see because it blends in with the color of the dark tree.

Answer the following questions about the picture above.

1. Which of the peppered moths is easier to see?

_____

_____

2. Why would predators eat more of the lighter colored peppered moths?

_____

_____

3. What would happen if the trees were much lighter in color? Why?

_____

_____

Animal Adaptations

Fill in the blanks.

Vocabulary

mimicry
heredity
diversity
coloration
crossbreeding
instinct
hybrids
camouflage

1. An animal that does not move, or moves very, very slowly, and looks like its surroundings is using _____ to protect itself.

2. The passing of inherited traits from parents to offspring is called _____.

3. Living things that have parents that are quite different from each other, such as donkeys and horses, are called _____.

4. Animal _____ refers to a group of the same kind of animal in which there are lots of animals with different traits.

5. Looking like something else is an example of _____.

6. Dark-colored moths that blend in with the background are an example of protective _____.

7. Mating closely related living things is a process called _____.

8. An inherited behavior that is done automatically is called _____.

Answer each question.

9. Explain why animals avoid a syrphid insect even though it doesn't sting. What kind of adaptation is this protection called?

_____

_____

10. How is a leaf butterfly protected from being eaten? What is this kind of protection called?

_____

_____

_____

©Macmillan/McGraw-Hill

Animal Adaptations

Vocabulary

background	shape	wings
camouflaged	protective	blending
adaptation	color	

Fill in the blanks.

An animal that does not move, or moves very, very slowly, and looks like its

surroundings is _____. Camouflage is another important

_____ that lets animals avoid their predators. There are two

basic kinds of camouflage, or _____ in with the environment.

One has to do with an animal's _____. The other has to do

with its _____. The _____ of the leaf butter-

fly are shaped like the leaves of a plant. Dark-colored peppered moths blend

in with the _____. This is an example of

_____ coloration.

Animal Diversity

Circle the letter of the best answer.

1. Living things that have parents that are different species are called
   - **a.** donkeys
   - **b.** hybrids
   - **c.** offspring
   - **d.** mules

2. A group of organs that work together to do a certain job is an
   - **a.** organ system
   - **b.** tissue
   - **c.** brain
   - **d.** cell

3. Animals that blend in with their backgrounds are an example of protective
   - **a.** hiding
   - **b.** camouflaging
   - **c.** coloration
   - **d.** mimicry

4. A trait that is passed down from one generation to the next is
   - **a.** inherited
   - **b.** mimicry
   - **c.** diversity
   - **d.** instinct

5. Animals that do not have backbones are
   - **a.** vertebrates
   - **b.** mammals
   - **c.** jellyfish
   - **d.** invertebrates

6. Camouflage is when
   - **a.** an animal looks like another animal.
   - **b.** an animal uses protective coloration.
   - **c.** an animal moves very, very slowly, and looks like its surroundings.
   - **d.** an animal looks like a thornbug.

Circle the letter of the best answer.

7. A tissue is a group of
   a. similar cells that have the same job or function.
   b. different organs that come together.
   c. invertebrates, either fish, birds, amphibians, reptiles, or mammals.
   d. vertebrates

8. An animal that looks like another in an unpleasant way is using
   a. protective coloration   b. camouflage
   c. mimicry   d. heredity

9. The passing of inherited traits from parents to offspring is called
   a. inherited   b. heredity
   c. coloration   d. mimicry

10. Mating closely related living things is a process called
    a. mimicry   b. inherited traits
    c. coloration   d. crossbreeding

11. Animals that have backbones are
    a. vertebrates   b. reptiles
    c. agnatha   d. invertebrates

12. A group of the same kind of animal in which there are lots of animals with different traits is called animal
    a. crossbreed   b. adaptation
    c. mimicry   d. diversity

13. A group of tissues that come together is a(n)
    a. organ   b. system
    c. cell   d. building block

© Macmillan/McGraw-Hill

Meanings and Words

Read each meaning. Then find a word in the Word Box that fits that meaning, and write it on the line.

Word Box

tropism	stimulus	system	heredity	camouflage
cambium	vertebrates	cotyledon	mimicry	chlorophyll
frond	embryo	organ	rhizoid	conifer

Meanings   **Words**

1. looking like something else _____

2. a green chemical in plants _____

3. separates the xylem from the phloem _____

4. blending in with the environment _____

5. anchors moss to the soil _____

6. animals that have backbones _____

7. the leaf of a fern _____

8. tissues of different kinds come together to make this _____

9. a tiny leaflike structure inside a seed _____

10. a group of organs that work together to do a certain job _____

11. something that makes a living thing react _____

12. a growth response _____

13. the passing of inherited traits from parents to offspring _____

14. immature plant inside a seed _____

15. a tree that produces seeds in cones _____

©Macmillan/McGraw-Hill

Word Webs

A word web lists words that describe or relate to the same thing. Here's an example using the word *bacteria*.

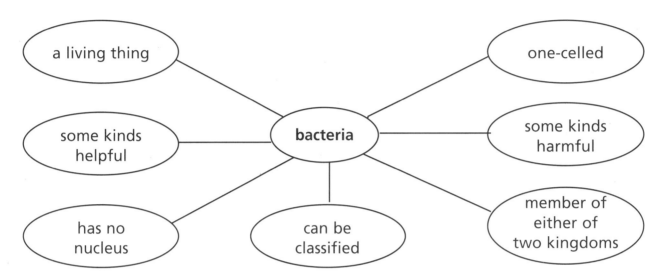

Now it's your turn. choose a vocabulary word, such as *conifer, tissue,* or *photosynthesis*. Make a web using other words that relate to or describe it.

Find-a-Word

Look across, down, and diagonally to find these hidden words:

ASK, BACTERIUM, CHLOROPHYLL, CLASSIFY, CORTEX, CYCAD, DICOT, FRONDS, FRUIT, HYPOTHESIS, MOSS, NUCLEUS, PHLOEM, PHOTOSYNTHESIS, PHYLUM, PLANTS, POLLEN, PROTIST, RESPIRATION, RHIZOID, RHIZOME, ROOTS, SEEDS, SPORE, STIMULUS, STOMATA, TREE, VARIABLE, VASCULAR, XYLEM.

P	P	O	L	L	E	N	Z	F	R	O	N	D	S	X
R	H	I	Z	O	M	E	J	X	F	R	U	I	T	Z
H	L	O	V	A	S	C	U	L	A	R	C	Z	O	J
I	O	X	T	C	Y	C	A	D	X	Y	L	E	M	C
Z	E	P	R	O	T	I	S	T	T	R	E	E	A	H
O	M	X	Z	J	S	T	I	M	U	L	U	S	T	L
I	V	J	K	P	H	Y	L	U	M	X	S	Z	A	O
D	A	S	Z	X	J	R	N	C	O	R	T	E	X	R
X	R	S	P	H	Y	P	O	T	H	E	S	I	S	O
Z	I	Z	E	O	Z	X	J	O	H	M	O	S	S	P
B	A	C	T	E	R	I	U	M	T	E	A	S	K	H
J	B	X	Z	J	D	E	C	L	A	S	S	I	F	Y
P	L	A	N	T	S	S	D	I	C	O	T	I	X	L
R	E	S	P	I	R	A	T	I	O	N	X	Z	S	L

©Macmillan/McGraw-Hill

Ecosystems

You can use a cycle diagram to show a sequence of events that repeats itself, such as the carbon cycle. After one loop of the cycle has been completed, the events in the cycle begin again.

The Carbon Cycle

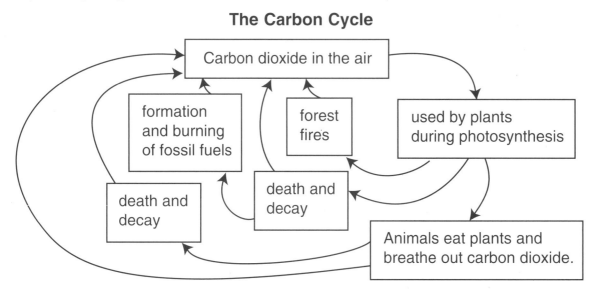

Complete the cycle diagram below for the water cycle. Two of the boxes have already been filled in.

The Water Cycle

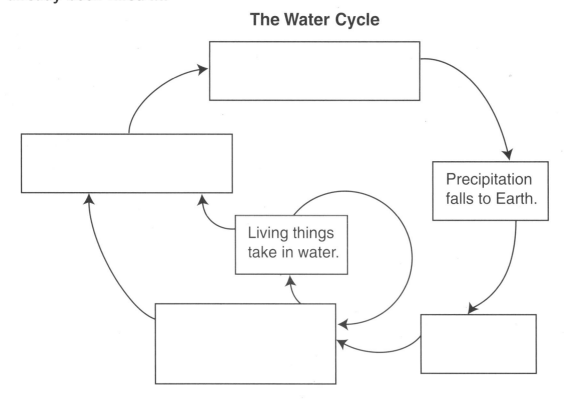

©Macmillan/McGraw-Hill

Sequence of Events

Study the following pictures to see how an abandoned farm becomes a forest. The pictures are not in the correct order. Read the captions and see if you can find clue words that will help you to put the pictures in the correct order.

The hot, dry field of tall weeds provides a perfect environment for pine seeds to sprout. Pine trees begin to grow and shade the weeds, which begin to die out. More birds join the community, as do small mammals like oppossums and skunks.

Tall weeds, such as aster, ragweed and goldenrod, and tall grasses grow among the crabgrass. The crabgrass can't easily survive in the shade cast by the taller weeds. It begins to die out. Rabbits and seed-eating birds move in.

The forest is now mostly deciduous trees. These trees are the habitats of many different kinds of birds and small animals, such as squirrels. Deer, raccoons, and foxes also live in the forest.

A community of crabgrass, insects, and mice invades the field where corn or another crop once grew.

A pine forest has replaced the old farm field. Yet the number of new pine seedlings drops because they can't grow in the shade. Seeds of deciduous trees such as maple, hickory, and oak sprout and take root. Larger animals like raccoons and foxes begin to visit.

©Macmillan/McGraw-Hill

Reading Diagrams

Nitrogen is a gas contained in Earth's atmosphere. Nitrogen is used to make the proteins that your body needs. However, animals and plants cannot use the nitrogen from the air to make their proteins. They must get nitrogen by eating proteins. The diagram below shows how nitrogen is cycled from the air to the soil, from the soil to the plants, and from the plants to the animals.

Ammonia   Nitrites   Nitrates   Nitrites and ammonia   Nitrogen compounds

Use the diagram to answer the following questions.

1. Describe three ways that nitrogen is introduced into the soil.

   _____

   _____

   _____

2. Where do you think most of the Earth's nitrogen is stored?

   _____

3. According to the diagram, could the nitrogen cycle work without the animals?

   _____

   _____

©Macmillan/McGraw-Hill

Living Things and Their Environment

Fill in the blanks. Reading Skill: **Sequence of Events** - questions 10, 11, 12

What Is an Ecosystem?

1. All the interacting living and nonliving things in an area describes a(n) _____.

2. The study of how everything in an ecosystem interacts in order to survive is called _____.

3. A nonliving factor in an ecosystem is called a(n) _____ factor.

4. Abiotic factors in an ecosystem include light, water, _____, temperature, air, and minerals.

5. Living things need _____, such as calcium, iron, and phosphorus.

6. Animals need _____ to produce the energy for their bodies.

7. The living parts of an ecosystem are called _____ factors.

8. Living organisms that produce oxygen and food that animals need are called _____.

9. Animals, or _____, produce the carbon dioxide that plants need.

10. Decomposers break down dead organisms and produce _____ that enrich the soil.

What Is a Prairie Ecosystem Like?

11. Long ago, the prairie was a "sea of wild _____."

12. Native Americans once hunted _____ on prairie lands. Today cattle and crops live there.

What Animals Live on the Blackland Prairie?

13. About _____ species of animals live on the Blackland Prairie.

14. Pipits, longspurs, horned larks, and about 300 other kinds of _____ live on the Blackland Prairie.

How Are Living Things Organized?

15. All the organisms of a species living in the same area make up a(n) _____.

16. All the populations of living organisms in an area make up a(n) _____.

What Are Niches and Habitats?

17. The place where an organism lives is called its _____.

18. What a species eats and what eats that species is part of its _____, or role in the ecosystem.

What Happens When Habitats Change?

19. The eastern spadefoot toad has hind feet shaped like spades so it can dig for _____ during a drought.

What Is the Treasure of the Blackland Prairie?

20. Prairie soils can often be identified by their rich, dark _____, or top layer of soil.

21. Partly decayed plant matter that enriches the prairie soil is called _____.

22. The nutrients in some prairie soils tend to stay near the _____ because low rainfall does not carry nutrients deep into the ground.

© Macmillan/McGraw-Hill

What Is an Ecosystem?

This diagram shows two different pictures of what could be a single environment. One picture focuses on abiotic factors and the other on biotic factors. The small drawings in each picture show close-ups of some of the smaller factors.

Abiotic factors in an ecosystem include light, water, soil, temperature, air, and minerals.

Biotic factors in an ecosystem include plants, animals, fungi, protists, and bacteria.

Answer these questions about the diagram above.

1. Name three biotic factors in the diagram.

_____

2. Name three abiotic factors in the diagram.

_____

3. What factors are in the biotic close-up?

_____

4. What factors are in the abiotic close-up?

_____

The Blackland Prairie

The Blackland Prairie is the largest remaining prairie in the United States. About 500 species of animals live on this prairie.

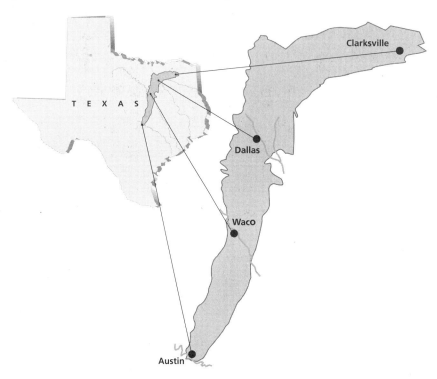

Answer the following questions about the map above.

1. Describe how the Blackland Prairie is situated within Texas.

   _____

   _____

2. Name three cities or towns within the Blackland Prairie.

   _____

   _____

3. What do most of the cities have in common in terms of the geographical features of their location?

   _____

   _____

©Macmillan/McGraw-Hill

Living Things and Their Environment

Vocabulary

a. ecosystem
b. ecology
c. biotic factor
d. abiotic factor
e. population
f. community
g. habitat
h. niche

Match the correct letter with the description.

_____ 1. a living part of an ecosystem

_____ 2. all the populations living in an area

_____ 3. a nonliving part of an ecosystem

_____ 4. all the living and nonliving things in an area that interact with each other

_____ 5. the role of an organism in its community

_____ 6. all the organisms of one species that live in an area at the same time

_____ 7. the area in which an organism lives

_____ 8. the study of how living things and their environment interact

A new shopping center, which covers the soil habitat of worms, is built. Identify the following factors in an ecosystem as biotic or abiotic.

9. a parking lot _____

10. worms _____

11. soil _____

12. new stores _____

Answer the following questions.

13. What will happen to the worms when the parking lot is poured?

_____

14. What is lost when the new stores are built? What is gained?

_____

_____

15. Birds eat worms. How does the new shopping center affect local birds?

_____

© Macmillan/McGraw-Hill

Living Things and Their Environment

Vocabulary

ecosystem	minerals	dioxide	ecology
abiotic	water	energy	food

Fill in the blanks.

All the living and nonliving things in an area interacting with each other is a(n) _____. The study of how living things and their environment interact is called _____. The nonliving parts of an ecosystem are _____ factors. All living things require _____ to stay alive. Living things also need _____ such as iron and calcium. Algae and plants must have sunlight to make _____. They also need carbon _____. Animals require oxygen to produce the _____ their bodies need.

Food Chains and Food Webs

Fill in the blanks. 📖 Reading Skill: **Sequence of Events** - questions 4, 16, 23

What Is a Food Chain?

1. All the energy in an ecosystem comes from the _____.

2. The energy of the Sun is stored in _____, which is passed from one organism to another.

3. The path that energy takes from producers to consumers to decomposers is called a(n) _____.

4. On a prairie, the food chains start with _____, which produce food during _____.

What Is a Food Web?

5. A food web shows the relationship between all _____ in a community.

6. Food chains overlap into a(n) _____.

7. Organisms that use the Sun's energy to make their own food are called _____.

8. In oceans, the main producers are _____.

9. Organisms that cannot make their own food are _____.

10. Consumers that eat producers are called _____.

11. Animals that eat other animals are called _____.

12. Living things that hunt other living things are _____.

13. Hunted animals are called _____.

14. _____ feed on the remains of dead animals instead of hunting.

15. Animals that eat both animals and plants are _____.

16. Food chains end with _____, which break down dead matter.

© Macmillan/McGraw-Hill

How Are Populations Connected?

17. A change in one _____ affects all the other organisms in that food chain.

18. Animals may be adapted to changes in their _____.

19. _____ help scientists predict how communities will be affected by change.

How Do Populations Adapt to Competition for Food?

20. Florida anoles were threatened when a new, bigger species of anole somehow arrived from _____.

21. The Florida anole found a new _____ high up in the treetops.

How Does Energy Move in a Community?

22. Energy is _____ as it passes from one organism to another in a food chain.

23. A(n) _____ shows there is less food at the top than at the bottom.

24. Scientists have determined that _____ percent of the energy is lost from one level of an energy pyramid to the next.

How Do Food Webs Affect You?

25. The ocean turns red when a group of algae called _____ bloom.

26. Poison from this algae can _____ fish and make humans sick.

What Is a Food Chain?

This illustration shows the members of a prairie food chain. You can see both producers and consumers. Identify where you think the food chain starts. Then follow the chain from one member to the next.

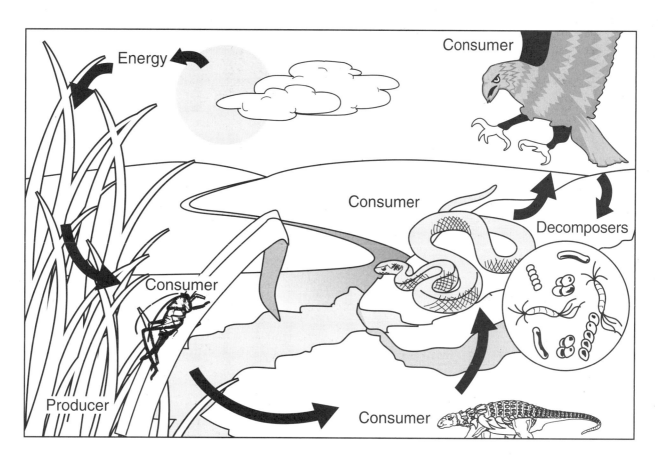

Answer these questions about the illustration above.

1. Where does the food chain start? _____

2. What producers are in the food chain? _____

3. What is the first consumer in the food chain? _____

4. What other consumers are in the food chain? _____

5. What is the direction of energy flow in this food chain?

_____

6. What happens to the hawk? _____

What Is a Food Web?

This diagram shows a food web. Arrows point from an organism to the organisms that consume it. Notice that there is more than one arrow pointing to most of the consumers. Energy flows from producers to consumers. Trace the direction of several arrows to see how energy flows through the web.

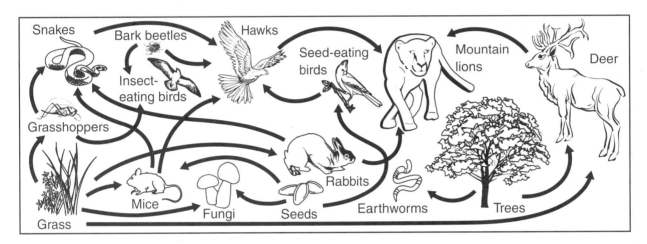

Answer these questions about the diagram above.

1. Does the arrow point to the eater or the one eaten?

   _____

2. What three producers do you see in this food web? _____

3. Why don't the producers have arrows pointing toward them?

   _____

   _____

4. Name three consumers you see.

   _____

5. What animals are not eaten by any other animal pictured in this food web?

   _____

6. What does the rabbit eat? What eats the rabbit?

   _____

Food Chains and Food Webs

Match the correct letter with the description.

_____ 1. the overlapping food chains in a community

_____ 2. a living thing that hunts other living things for food

_____ 3. an animal that feeds on the remains of dead animals

_____ 4. the original source of energy in an ecosystem

_____ 5. the path of energy in food from one organism to another

_____ 6. an animal that eats only other animals

_____ 7. an animal that eats both plants and animals

_____ 8. a living thing that is hunted for food

_____ 9. an animal that eats only plants

Vocabulary

a. food chain

b. food web

c. herbivore

d. carnivore

e. predator

f. prey

g. scavenger

h. omnivore

i. Sun

Define the following and match the example(s) from the column of organisms.

9. producers _____

_____

10. consumers _____

_____

11. decomposers _____

_____

a. cows

b. humans

c. plants

d. bacteria

Answer the following questions.

12. Describe where plants, humans, and cows would be located on an energy pyramid.

top _____ middle _____ bottom _____

13. Which level of the energy pyramid has the most organisms?

_____

14. What would happen if suddenly all the cows disappeared?

_____

_____

©Macmillan/McGraw-Hill

Food Chains and Food Webs

Vocabulary

carnivores	producers	omnivores	decomposers
scavengers	hunt	overlap	the Sun
herbivores	consumers	web	

Fill in the blanks.

In communities, organisms compete for food. This competition means that many small food chains in an ecosystem may _____ each other. This creates a food _____. All food webs have _____, which make their own food. They rely on _____ for energy. Organisms that cannot make their own food are called _____. Some, such as grasshoppers, are _____, which eat producers. Others, like cats, are _____, which eat other animals. Predators _____ other living things called prey for food. Some meat eaters known as _____ eat the remains of dead animals. People are _____ because they eat both plants and animals. Every food chain and food web ends with _____, which break down wastes.

©Macmillan/McGraw-Hill

Cycles of Life

Fill in the blanks. Reading Skill: **Sequence of Events** - question 10

What Is the Water Cycle?

1. Heat energy makes water _____ and rise into the air.

2. When cooled enough, water vapor _____ into tiny water droplets.

3. Droplets that become so large and heavy that they can no longer stay up in the air fall to Earth's surface as _____.

4. Water stored in soil and rock is _____.

5. Water flowing downhill across the surface of Earth is called _____.

6. The process of naturally recycling water on Earth is called the _____.

7. Plants give some of their water back to the atmosphere through their _____.

How Are Trees Recycled?

8. Dead trees provide _____ that other trees need.

9. Organisms that recycle matter in dead organisms are called _____.

10. Decomposers break down dead wood into carbon dioxide and _____, which contains nitrogen.

11. Nitrogen is found in _____, substances that add _____ to the soil.

What Is the Carbon Cycle?

12. The gas added to the air by decaying organisms, breathing animals, and burning fossil fuels is _____.

13. Plants use carbon to make sugars, starches, and proteins during _____.

14. Animals use the carbon in sugars, starches, and proteins to make their own _____.

How Is Nitrogen Recycled?

15. Animals get nitrogen by eating _____.

16. Plants get nitrogen by absorbing it from the _____.

17. The way nitrogen moves between the air, soil, plants, and animals is called the _____.

18. Decomposers break down the proteins of dead plants into the nitrogen-containing substance _____.

19. Soil bacteria change ammonia into _____.

20. Animal wastes contain _____ compounds.

21. Plants use nitrogen to make _____.

22. Nitrates are turned back into nitrogen gas by _____.

Why Recycle?

23. Sunlight is a(n) _____ resource.

24. The building blocks of products are _____.

25. A resource that can be replaced, like a tree, is _____.

What Is the Carbon Cycle?

This illustration uses arrows to show how carbon cycles through the environment. Follow the arrows to see how carbon moves. Notice how the arrows form circles.

Trees

Carbon dioxide

Trees

Plants take in carbon dioxide and give off oxygen which animals use.

Carbon Carbon enters the air when plants and animals decay. It enters the air when animals breathe out. It enters the air when fossil fuels such as coal, oil, gasoline, and natural gas are burned.

Animals Animals eat plant sugars, starches, proteins, and other substances. The carbon in these substances is used by animals to make their own body chemicals.

Oxygen

Car exhaust

Death, Decay, Storage When living things die, decay releases the carbon compounds in their bodies. Some of it is turned into carbon dioxide by decomposers. Over millions of years some of it turns into fossil fuels.

Photosynthesis During photosynthesis plants use the carbon from carbon dioxide to make sugars, starches, and proteins.

Oil

Decaying matter

Answer these questions about the illustration above.

1. What sources of carbon dioxide are shown?

_____

2. What takes in carbon dioxide? _____

3. How do animals use carbon? _____

4. Why is there an arrow from the plant to decaying matter?

_____

5. Why does car exhaust release carbon dioxide? _____

_____

How Is Nitrogen Recycled?

This diagram shows the nitrogen cycle. Begin at the cow and trace the arrows as you describe what is happening in your own words.

Air Air is made up of about 78 percent nitrogen gas.

Denitrifying Bacteria Some soil bacteria turn nitrates back into nitrogen gas.

Plants Plants absorb nitrates dissolved in water through their roots. The nitrogen is then used by the plant to make proteins.

Animals Animals eat plant proteins, or they eat other animals that eat plant proteins. Animal wastes contain nitrogen compounds.

Ammonia   Nitrites   Nitrates   Nitrites and ammonia   Nitrogen compounds

Decomposers When the plant dies, decomposers in the soil break down the plant proteins. One product is the nitrogen-containing substance ammonia. Soil bacteria change ammonia into nitrites.

Nitrogen-Fixing Bacteria Some bacteria that grow on pea and bean roots give those plants the nitrogen they need. The bacteria turn nitrogen gas in the air to nitrogen-containing substances the plants can use to make their proteins.

Bacteria Certain bacteria can use nitrogen from the air to make nitrogen-containing substances called *nitrites*. Other bacteria can turn nitrites into *nitrates*—another group of nitrogen-containing substances.

Answer these questions about the diagram above.

1. What nitrogen compounds can bacteria make? _____

2. Where do plants get nitrates from? _____

   _____

   _____

3. How does the cow rely on plants? _____

   _____

4. How does nitrogen leave an animal's body? _____

5. What organism turns nitrates back into nitrogen gas? _____

Cycles of Life

Match the correct letter with the description.

_____ 1. any form of water that falls to Earth

_____ 2. the process in which a gas changes into a liquid

_____ 3. the continuous transfer of carbon between the atmosphere and living things

_____ 4. water in its gas state

_____ 5. the continuous movement of water between Earth's surface and the air

_____ 6. the transfer of nitrogen between the atmosphere and soil, plants, and animals

_____ 7. the process in which a liquid changes into a gas

Identify which cycle—water, nitrogen, or carbon—is linked to each term.

8. precipitation _____   9. fertilizers _____

10. ammonia _____   11. exhaust _____

12. bacteria _____   13. condensation _____

14. photosynthesis_____   15. oxygen _____

16. runoff _____   17. evaporation _____

18. proteins _____   18. fossil fuels _____

Describe one way animals are part of each of the three cycles.

20. water cycle _____

_____

21. carbon cycle _____

_____

22. nitrogen cycle _____

_____

Cycles of Life

Vocabulary

oceans	hail	cycle	precipitation
Sun	runoff	clouds	groundwater

Fill in the blanks.

In nature, water continuously moves between Earth's surface and the air in a process called the water _____. Most of Earth's water is contained in _____. Energy from the _____ evaporates water, making it rise. Some water droplets and ice crystals form _____. When these grow large and heavy, the water falls to Earth's surface as _____. This can take the form of snow, rain, _____, or sleet. Water can be stored as _____ or it can flow as _____.

Ecosystems

Circle the letter of the best answer.

1. All the living and nonliving things in an area interacting with each other describes a(n)
   a. community.
   b. ecosystem.
   c. habitat.
   d. population.

2. The study of how living things and their environment interact is
   a. biology.
   b. earth science.
   c. ecology.
   d. geology.

3. A living part of a system is what kind of factor?
   a. abiotic
   b. biotic
   c. predator
   d. prey

4. All the organisms of one species that live in an area at the same time is a(n)
   a. community.
   b. ecology.
   c. ecosystem.
   d. population.

5. All the populations living in an area describes a(n)
   a. community.
   b. ecosystem.
   c. niche.
   d. population.

6. The area in which an organism lives is its
   a. population.
   b. food web.
   c. habitat.
   d. niche.

7. The role an organism has in its ecosystem is its
   a. community.
   b. food chain.
   c. habitat.
   d. niche.

8. The path of energy in food from one organism to another is a
   a. food chain.
   b. food cycle.
   c. food web.
   d. niche.

9. An animal that eats both plants and animals is a(n)
   a. abiotic factor.
   b. carnivore.
   c. herbivore.
   d. omnivore.

10. A living thing that is hunted for food is called
    a. a carnivore.
    b. an omnivore.
    c. a predator.
    d. prey.

11. An animal that feeds on the remains of dead animals is
    a. an omnivore.
    b. a predator.
    c. prey.
    d. a scavenger.

12. Precipitation is part of the
    a. carbon cycle.
    b. food cycle.
    c. nitrogen cycle.
    d. water cycle.

13. Photosynthesis is part of the
    a. carbon cycle.
    b. food cycle.
    c. nitrogen cycle.
    d. water cycle.

14. Bacteria play an important role in the
    a. carbon cycle.
    b. food cycle.
    c. nitrogen cycle.
    d. water cycle.

Chapter Summary

1. What is the name of the chapter you just finished reading?

   _____

   _____

2. What are four vocabulary words you learned in the chapter?
   Write a definition for each.

   _____

   _____

   _____

   _____

   _____

   _____

   _____

   _____

3. What are two main ideas that you learned in this chapter?

   _____

   _____

   _____

   _____

   _____

   _____

Populations and Ecosystems

You can use a concept map to summarize information. The top oval of this concept map contains a general topic. Lower ovals contain more specific concepts related to the general topic. The ovals are connected by linking words like "in which" or "such as." If you follow a line of concepts and links down the map, you will see that they usually form a sentence. The concept map below summarizes information related to symbiosis. The links and some of the ovals have already been completed for you. Fill in the remaining ovals.

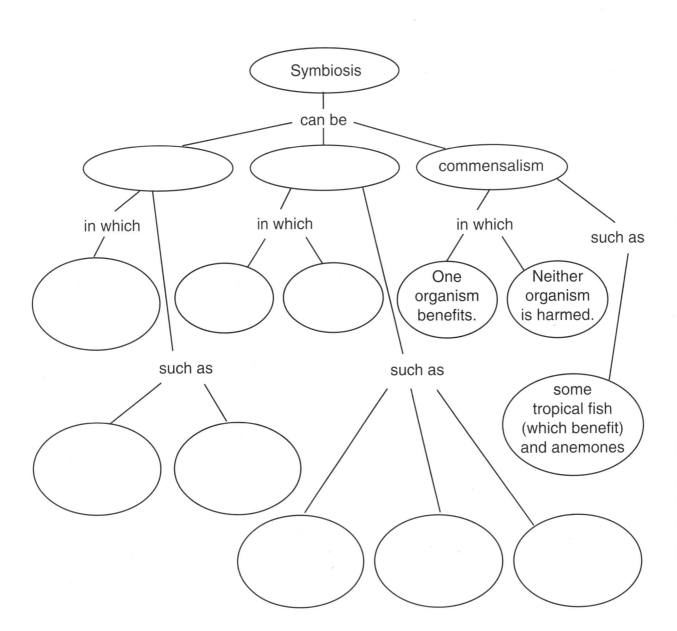

©Macmillan/McGraw-Hill

Summarize

A summary tells only the most important parts of a story. Usually, one or two sentences are enough to give a reader an idea of what the story will be about.

Read the following text based on the information in your textbook. Then summarize it in one or two sentences.

What Is Symbiosis?

Organisms interact with each other in different ways. Some organisms are predators and some are prey. However, there are also other kinds of relationships between organisms.

Symbiosis is a relationship between two kinds of organisms that lasts over a period of time. Sometimes both organisms benefit from the relationship. Sometimes one organism benefits while harming the other. Sometimes only one benefits, while the other is not affected.

When a relationship benefits both organisms, it is called mutualism. Parasitism is when one organism, the parasite, lives on or in another organism called the host. The parasite benefits from the relationship while the host is harmed by it. A relationship in which one organism benefits from another without harming or helping it is called commensalism.

My Summary:

_____

_____

_____

_____

_____

© Macmillan/McGraw-Hill

Write a Summary

**Read the following text based on the information in your textbook.
Then summarize it in one or two sentences.**

What Happens When There Is a Red Tide?

"Ocean Blooms on the Increase off Texas Coast" might not seem like a frightening headline, yet to an ecologist it means trouble. The "blooms" refer to an increase in the population of microscopic sea organisms called fire algae. They get their name from their red color. When they bloom, they turn hundreds of square miles of ocean red.

Dinoflagellates, or algae, are the lowest part of the ocean food web and are at the base of every ocean energy pyramid. The algae store the Sun's energy, which is passed up through the pyramid.

However, some algae, like the fire algae, create poisons. People who live close to the water along the Gulf Coast of the United States might get their first hint of a red tide when their throats and noses start to sting. This happens because the poisons produced by the fire algae can come in on sea breezes.

In the sea, small fish and mussels feed on algae. The fire algae's poison can kill the fish. This reduces the energy or food available to consumers higher up in the food chain. The poison can also kill consumers higher on the food chain. In 1991 many California pelicans died after eating anchovies that had eaten fire algae.

My Summary:

_____

_____

_____

_____

©Macmillan/McGraw-Hill

How Populations Survive

Fill in the blanks. Reading Skill: **Summarize** - questions 2, 23

What Controls the Growth of Populations?

1. Anything that controls the growth or survival of a population is called a(n) _____.

2. Limiting factors like temperature, sunlight, and water are _____.

3. The number of predators an ecosystem can support is determined by the number of _____.

4. A population's size can limit its _____.

How Do Plants Adapt to Harsh Environments?

5. Plants have developed special characteristics called _____ to help them survive.

6. One of the harshest areas for plant growth is a(n) _____.

7. The barrel cactus has _____ roots so it can quickly soak up rainwater.

8. The barrel cactus can store water in its _____.

What Is Symbiosis?

9. In nature a relationship between two kinds of organisms that lasts over a period of time is called _____.

10. When a relationship between two kinds of organisms benefits both of them, it is called _____.

11. One example of mutualism is the relationship between the Joshua tree and the _____.

12. In protecting its eggs, the moth also _____ the yucca flower so it can make seeds.

©Macmillan/McGraw-Hill

13. Some of these seeds sprout into new _____.

14. When the eggs hatch into _____ they feed on some of the seeds.

What Is Parasitism?

15. A relationship in which one kind of organism lives on or in another organism and may harm that organism is called _____.

16. Organisms that live on or in other organisms are called _____.

17. The organisms they feed on are called _____.

18. Dogs and cats are often hosts to parasites called _____.

What Is Commensalism?

19. The relationship where one organism benefits from another without harming or helping it is called _____.

20. An example of this kind of relationship is _____ attaching themselves to tall trees high above the rain forest floor.

How Do Populations Survive Earth's Changes?

21. Cold periods in which vast ice sheets covered the land are called _____.

22. About 65 million years ago a(n) _____ hit Earth.

23. The impact may have caused large animals, like _____, to die out because there weren't enough plants.

How Do People Change the Environment?

24. About 15 times a minute you change the environment by _____.

25. Each time you exhale, you add _____ and _____ to the air.

©Macmillan/McGraw - Hill

The Barrel Cactus

The picture below shows cacti in their native environment, the Sonoran Desert. The conditions in the desert are harsh compared to other biomes. Plants and animals have to compete for the scarce water supply. This competition has caused the species that live in the desert to make adaptations to survive.

Answer the following questions about the picture above.

1. In what way does the soil pictured increase the harshness of the conditions for desert plants?

   _____

   _____

2. How do the cacti in the picture differ from the leafy plants shown?

   _____

   _____

   _____

3. What kinds of adaptations has the barrel cactus made which allow it to grow much larger than the other plants pictured?

   _____

   _____

How Do Populations Survive Earth's Changes?

This drawing shows an event that scientists think happened in Earth's history.

Scientific evidence suggests that about 65 million years ago, an asteroid (larger than shown) from outer space may have struck Earth, killing off many animals and plants.

Answer these questions about the drawing above.

1. How long ago did this event occur?

_____

2. What is hurtling toward Earth? _____

3. What organisms are on the ground?

_____

4. What happened to the meteorite? _____

5. What effect did the meteorite have on Earth?

_____

How Populations Survive

Match the correct letter with the description.

_____ 1. a relationship between two kinds of organisms that benefits one without harming or helping the other

_____ 2. a characteristic that helps an organism survive in its environment

_____ 3. a relationship between two kinds of organisms that benefits both

_____ 4. anything that controls the growth or survival of an organism or population

_____ 5. a relationship in which one kind of organism lives on or in another organism and may harm that organism

_____ 6. a relationship between two kinds of organisms over time

Vocabulary

a. limiting factor

b. adaptation

c. symbiosis

d. mutualism

e. parasitism

f. commensalism

Identify the following limiting factors as biotic or abiotic.

7. sunlight _____

8. grass _____

9. hawk _____

10. temperature _____

11. insects _____

12. water _____

Answer the following questions.

13. Describe how you affect the world's environment simply by breathing.

_____

_____

14. How is the barrel cactus adapted to its environment?

_____

_____

How Populations Survive

pollinates	symbosis	hosts
harm	sea anemones	fleas
commensalism	mutualism	eggs

Fill in the blanks.

Different kinds of organisms interact with each other in a number of different ways. In nature a relationship between two kinds of organisms that lasts over a period of time is called _____. When a relationship between two kinds of organisms benefits both of them, it is called _____. For example, the yucca moth _____ the yucca flower, and the yucca flower provides a place for yucca moth _____ to develop. A relationship in which one kind of organism lives on or in another organism and may _____ that organism is called parasitism. The organisms parasites feed on are called _____. Dogs and cats have parasites called _____. A relationship where one organism benefits from another without helping or harming it is called _____. Certain tropical fish live unharmed among the poisonous tentacles of _____ _____, which provide safety for the fish.

Biomes

Fill in the blanks. Reading Skill: **Summarize** - questions 10, 22

What Is a Biome?

1. The six major kinds of large ecosystems are called _____.

2. Rich topsoil over clay is found in the _____.

3. Acidic soil with a surface of decayed pine needles describes the _____.

4. A biome with nutrient-poor soil near the equator is the _____.

5. You would find a soil poor in animal and plant decay products, but rich in minerals in a(n) _____.

6. Nutrient-poor soil and permafrost are found in the _____.

7. Rich topsoil and few trees characterize a(n) _____.

What Are Grasslands?

8. Prairies and savannas are two types of _____.

9. Grasslands in the United States are _____, meaning mild.

10. Grasslands are called the _____ of the world because they produce so much wheat, corn, and oats.

What Is the Taiga Like?

11. Lakes and ponds in the taiga were formed by moving _____.

12. Taigas are mostly _____ forests.

What Is the Tundra?

13. The biome located between the taiga and the polar ice sheets is the _____.

14. Permanently frozen soil, or _____, keeps water from flowing downward.

What Is the Desert Biome Like?

15. A sandy biome with little precipitation and plant life is a(n) _____.

16. Every continent has a desert, but the _____ in Africa is the largest.

What Is a Deciduous Forest?

17. Many trees lose their leaves each year in a(n) _____.

18. The word "deciduous" means _____ to the ground.

What Are Tropical Rain Forests?

19. Tropical rain forests are near Earth's _____.

20. Little sunlight reaches the ground in a tropical rain forest because of the thick _____.

21. Most of the life in a tropical rain forest is high up in the _____.

What Are Water Ecosystems Like?

22. The main difference between Earth's water ecosystems is _____.

23. Organisms that float on the water are called _____.

24. Organisms that swim through the water are _____.

25. Organisms that dwell on the bottom are _____.

26. Crabs, mussels, and barnacles live in the _____ zone.

27. Photosynthetic organisms cannot live in the _____ region of the ocean because there is no sunlight.

Can Humans Change Ecosystems?

28. Many species of whales are threatened with _____.

29. Whales were used for food, oil, and _____.

30. The United States banned citizens from buying products made from whales in _____.

What Is a Biome?

Maps like this one show one aspect of Earth. In this case, biomes are highlighted. Make sure you look at how each biome is indicated. Then read the map to see where various biomes can be found.

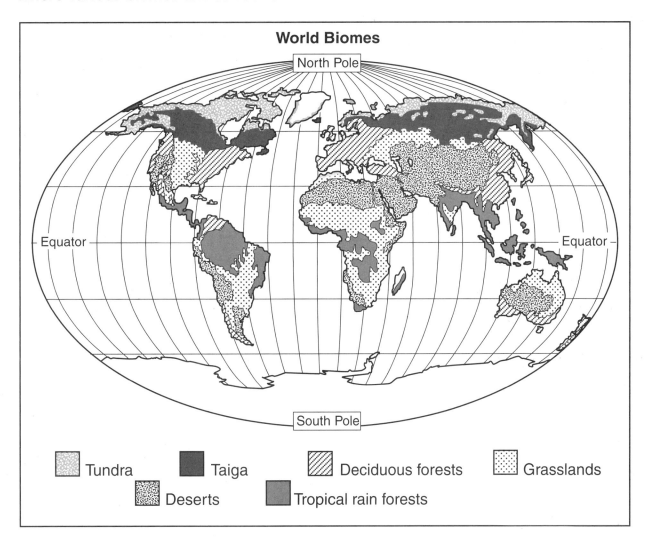

World Biomes

North Pole

Equator

Equator

South Pole

■ Tundra ■ Taiga ▨ Deciduous forests ▦ Grasslands

▨ Deserts ■ Tropical rain forests

Study the map of biomes and answer the questions below.

1. What biome is found near the equator? _____

2. What biome stretches across northern Africa? _____

3. What biome is found just below the North Pole? _____

4. What are the three main biomes found in the United States?

_____

5. What biome do you live in? _____

© Macmillan/McGraw-Hill

What are Water Ecosystems Like?

This illustration shows the kind of life at different levels of the ocean. Make sure you can identify each of the organisms in the picture as well as the three main layers.

Study the illustration and answer the questions below.

1. Which layer has waves?

   _____

   _____

2. How do waves affect plankton?

   _____

   _____

3. Which nekton live where the ocean floor is sometimes uncovered as waves move out?

   _____

   _____

4. In which layer are bacteria that live in boiling water found?

   _____

   _____

5. Which organisms get more sunlight—plankton or the bacteria that live in boiling water?

   _____

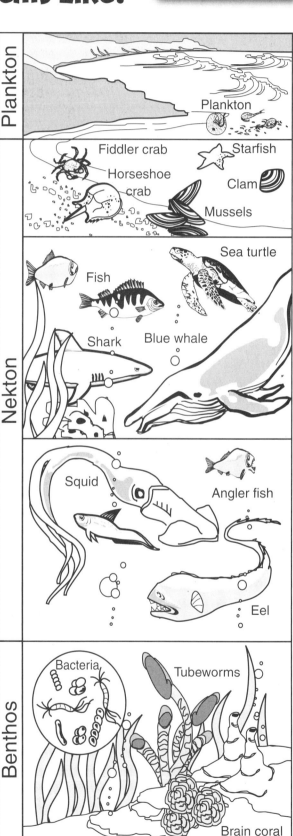

Plankton

Plankton

Fiddler crab

Starfish

Horseshoe crab

Clam

Mussels

Nekton

Sea turtle

Fish

Shark

Blue whale

Squid

Angler fish

Eel

Benthos

Bacteria

Tubeworms

Brain coral

© Macmillan/McGraw-Hill

Biomes

Match the correct letter with the description.

_____ 1. a forest biome with many kinds of trees that lose their leaves each autumn

_____ 2. one of Earth's large ecosystems, with its climate, soil, plants, and animals

_____ 3. a hot, humid biome near the equator, with much rainfall and a wide variety of life

_____ 4. a cold, treeless biome of the far north, marked by spongy topsoil

_____ 5. most lakes, streams, rivers, and ponds

_____ 6. a sandy or rocky biome, with little precipitation and little plant life

_____ 7. a cool, forest biome of conifers in the upper Northern Hemisphere

_____ 8. have tides, an upper region with many fish and whales, and a dark bottom

a. biome

b. taiga

c. tundra

d. desert

e. deciduous forest

f. tropical rain forest

g. freshwater ecosystems

h. saltwater ecosystems

Identify the biome described by each of the following.

9. few plants live on its floor because little sunlight penetrates the thick canopy

_____

10. plants grow deep roots to find scarce water _____

11. small plants have shallow roots and short growing seasons because of the permafrost _____

12. rainfall is irregular and much of this biome has been turned into farmlands

_____

13. mostly conifer trees in a cool climate _____

14. leaves turn color and fall during autumn _____

15. has boiling vents on the dark floor _____

16. where frogs, turtles, and brook trout live _____

Biomes

Vocabulary

minerals	leaves	tundra	taiga
permafrost	grasslands	plants	biomes

Fill in the blanks.

Six major ecosystems, or _____, are located around Earth. The desert has soil that is rich in _____. Prairie dogs and snakes live in American _____. The cold biome in the far north is the _____. Here, a layer of permanently frozen soil called _____ keeps water from flowing downward. The greatest diversity of _____ can be found in tropical rain forests. Mostly conifers grow in the _____. Deciduous forests have many different trees that lose their _____ each autumn.

How Ecosystems Change

Fill in the blanks. 📖 Reading Skill: **Summarize** - questions 4, 10

How Do Ecosystems Change?

1. _____ has a way of changing an ecosystem or producing a new one.

2. In Cambodia, abandoned cities have turned back into _____.

3. Over many years, an abandoned farm can turn into a(n) _____.

How Do Communities Change?

4. The gradual replacement of one community by another is _____.

5. Ecological succession in a place where a community already exists is called _____.

6. Where communities have been wiped out, _____ can begin.

7. A year after Mount Saint Helens erupted, you could find the rose-purple _____ of fireweed in the rubble.

8. The first species to be living in an otherwise lifeless area is a(n) _____.

9. A new community is called a(n) _____.

What Happens to Pioneer Communities?

10. Over many years, _____, _____, and _____ can break down rock into soil.

11. The final stage of succession is the _____.

12. After a major event, the processes of _____ begin all over again.

What's Living on Surtsey?

13. Surtsey is off the coast of _____.

14. Surtsey was formed by a(n) _____ in 1963.

15. Between 1963 and 1996, at least _____ types of plants were growing on Surtsey.

How Do Changes Affect Populations?

16. About six million years ago, fish and other sea creatures disappeared from the _____.

17. Fossils from a slightly later period reveal that _____ from Africa arrived in Europe.

18. Fossils of fish from _____ years ago turned up in the Mediterranean area.

19. Scientists think that Africa and Europe bumped each other at the _____.

20. This collision created a natural _____ between the Atlantic Ocean and the Mediterranean Sea.

21. The sea became a(n) _____ and fish and other marine life died out.

22. About five million years ago, the dam crumbled and water, carrying _____, made the Mediterranean a sea again.

Can Human Events Change Environments?

23. Rocks hold many useful _____.

24. Strip mining is one way to get rocks that are near the _____.

25. Strip mining harms living things because of water and air _____.

© Macmillan/McGraw-Hill

How Do Ecosystems Change?

These five pictures show the same place at five different times. By comparing pictures you can see how the environment has changed over a period of 100 years. Look at each picture and identify the different plants and animals.

Abandoned farm-first year

Second and third years

Four to six years later

Twenty-five years later

One hundred years later

Use the pictures above to answer these questions.

1. What kinds of plants do you see in the first picture? _____

2. What happens to these plants? _____

3. How do the animals change through the years?

   _____

4. How do the plants change through the years?

   _____

5. How many years pass before birds come to the area? _____

©Macmillan/McGraw-Hill

Stages of Succession

These pictures focus on how a small part of an ecosystem changes over time.
The pictures show how one thing gradually replaces another.

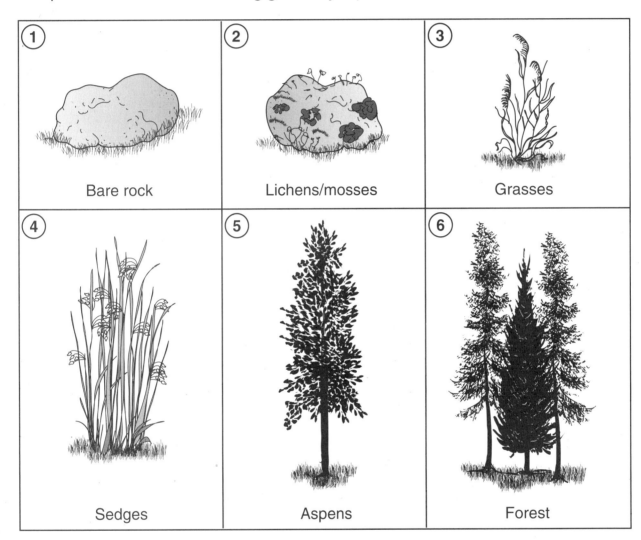

① Bare rock
② Lichens/mosses
③ Grasses
④ Sedges
⑤ Aspens
⑥ Forest

Use the pictures above to answer these questions.

1. What is the item in the first picture? _____

2. What is the difference between the rock in the first and second pictures?

   _____

3. What happens to the rock? _____

4. What do the aspens replace? _____

5. What is shown in the final picture? _____

How Ecosystems Change

Match the correct letter with the description.

_____ 1. the first species living in an area

_____ 2. the gradual replacement of one community
by another

_____ 3. ecological succession in a place where a community
already exists

_____ 4. the first community living in an area

_____ 5. ecological succession that happens where there
are few, if any, living things

_____ 6. the final stage of succession in an area, unless
a major change happens

Vocabulary

a. ecological
succession

b. pioneer
species

c. pioneer
community

d. climax
community

e. primary
succession

f. secondary
succession

Complete the table by listing one early change and one later change that took place following each event.

What Happened	Early Change	Later Change
farm abandoned	7.	8.
volcanic eruption	9.	10.
new building	11.	12.
continents bump	13.	14.

Answer the following questions.

15. How can changes in one ecosystem affect another ecosystem?

_____

16. Name three things you can do to help ecosystems.

_____

How Ecosystems Change

Vocabulary

forest	pioneer	secondary succession	eruption
primary succession	succession	fire	pioneer

Fill in the blanks.

The gradual replacement of one community by another is called ecological

_____. When a community begins where another community

already exists, _____ occurs. For example, a(n)

_____ can gradually replace a farm. When a community

begins where there are few, if any, living things, _____

occurs. Such places include land swept clean by a volcanic

_____ or forest _____. The first species to be

living in an otherwise lifeless area is a(n) _____ species. A

new community is also known as a(n) _____ community.

©Macmillan/McGraw-Hill

Populations and Ecosystems

Circle the letter of the best answer.

1. Anything that controls the growth or survival of an organism or population is a(n)
   a. abiotic factor.
   b. adaptation.
   c. biotic factor.
   d. limiting factor.

2. A characteristic that helps an organism survive in its environment is a(n)
   a. abiotic factor.
   b. adaptation.
   c. biotic factor.
   d. limiting factor.

3. A relationship between two kinds of organisms over time is
   a. commensalism.
   b. mutualism.
   c. parasitism.
   d. symbiosis.

4. A relationship between two kinds of organisms that benefits both is
   a. commensalism.
   b. mutualism.
   c. parasitism.
   d. symbiosis.

5. A relationship between two kinds of organisms that benefits one without harming the other is
   a. commensalism.
   b. mutualism.
   c. parasitism.
   d. symbiosis.

6. One of Earth's large ecosystems, with its climate, soil, plants, and animals, is a
   a. biome.
   b. climax community.
   c. pioneer community.
   d. taiga.

7. A cool, forest biome of conifers in the upper Northern Hemisphere is a
   a. deciduous forest.
   b. taiga.
   c. tropical rain forest.
   d. tundra.

© Macmillan/McGraw-Hill

8. A sandy or rocky biome, with little precipitation and little plant life, is a
   a. desert.
   b. pioneer community.
   c. taiga.
   d. tundra.

9. A forest biome with many kinds of trees that lose their leaves each autumn is a
   a. deciduous forest.
   b. taiga.
   c. tropical rain forest.
   d. tundra.

10. A hot, humid biome near the equator, with much rainfall and a wide variety of life, is a
    a. deciduous forest.
    b. taiga.
    c. tropical rain forest.
    d. tundra.

11. The gradual replacement of one community by another is called
    a. commensalism.
    b. ecological succession.
    c. pioneer succession.
    d. symbiosis.

12. The first species living in an area is the
    a. climax species.
    b. ecological succession.
    c. pioneer species.
    d. taiga.

13. The first community living in an area is the
    a. climax community.
    b. ecological community.
    c. pioneer community.
    d. premier community.

14. The final stage of succession in an area, unless a major change happens, is the
    a. climax community.
    b. ecological community.
    c. pioneer community.
    d. secondary community.

© Macmillan/McGraw-Hill

Name That Word

Use the words in the box to fill in the blanks.

Word Box				
carnivore	population	biotic factor	herbivore	food chain
ecological succession		niche	adaptation	scavenger
carbon dioxide		prey	habitat	

1. These words identify a living part of an ecosystem.

   _____

2. These words identify the movement of food energy from one organism to another. _____

3. This word identifies an organism's role in an ecosystem.

   _____

4. This word identifies a plant eater. _____

5. This word identifies all the members of a species in an area.

   _____

6. These words identify a compound needed by all living plants to make sugars.

   _____

7. This word identifies a meat eater. _____

8. This identifies the gradual replacement of one community by another.

   _____

9. This word identifies a meat eater that eats the remains of dead animals.

   _____

10. This word identifies a living thing hunted as food. _____

11. This word identifies where a population lives._____

12. This word identifies a characteristic that helps a living thing survive in its environment._____

Correct-a-Word

One word in each sentence below is wrong. Cross it out, and write the correct word above it. Use the Word Box to check your spelling.

Word Box				
deciduous	precipitation	ecology	decomposer	nitrogen
ecosystem	scavengers	pioneer	habitat	niche

1. Noxrogen is an element that all plants need for growth.

2. A primitive species is the first species to be living in an otherwise lifeless area.

3. Scallywags are meat eaters that eat the remains of dead animals.

4. An echovalley includes all the living and nonliving things in an environment.

5. The place where a population lives is a haberole.

6. Its nick is an organism's role in an ecosystem.

7. A producer is fungus or bacterium that breaks down dead plants and animals.

8. Deciding trees lose leaves in fall.

9. Precession is the rain, sleet, snow, or hail that falls to Earth.

10. Economy is the study of the interaction of living things and their environment.

Find-a-Word

Look across, down, and diagonally to find these hidden words:

ABIOTIC, ADAPT, AMMONIA, ANIMALS, AREA, BENTHOS, BIOME, CARBON, CARNIVORE, CHAIN, COMMUNITY, CONSUMER, DECIDUOUS, DESERT, EAT, ECOLOGY, ECOSYSTEM, FOOD, GAS, GRASSLAND, GROWTH, HERBIVORE, NEKTON, NICHE, NITROGEN, OMNIVORE, PARASITE, PLANKTON, PLANTS, POPULATION, PREY, PRODUCER, ROLE, SCAVENGER, SOIL, SPECIES, SURVIVE, SYMBIOSIS, TAIGA, TIDE, TUNDRA, WEB.

A	D	A	P	T	Z	S	Y	M	B	I	O	S	I	S	A
E	C	O	L	O	G	Y	Q	A	B	I	O	T	I	C	N
Q	C	C	Z	J	D	E	C	I	D	U	O	U	S	A	I
P	R	O	D	U	C	E	R	S	O	I	L	M	Q	V	M
O	S	N	S	G	R	A	S	S	L	A	N	D	E	E	A
P	U	S	I	Y	E	Q	B	E	N	T	H	O	S	N	L
U	R	U	P	C	S	A	Z	D	E	S	E	R	T	G	S
L	V	M	A	A	H	T	T	U	N	D	R	A	W	E	B
A	I	E	R	R	F	E	E	C	A	R	B	O	N	R	A
T	V	R	A	E	C	O	M	M	U	N	I	T	Y	G	M
I	E	Z	S	A	P	R	O	L	E	E	V	A	C	R	M
O	M	N	I	V	O	R	E	D	T	K	O	I	H	O	O
N	N	I	T	R	O	G	E	N	I	T	R	G	A	W	N
Z	S	P	E	C	I	E	S	Y	D	O	E	A	I	T	I
C	A	R	N	I	V	O	R	E	E	N	J	S	N	H	A
P	L	A	N	K	T	O	N	J	X	P	L	A	N	T	S

Rocks and Minerals

You can use a flowchart to show a sequence of events, such as the erosion of rock by ice. The first event is written in a box. The second event is written in a second box, and so on until all the events are listed. The boxes are then connected with arrows to show the order in which the events occur. Look at the example below showing how ice erodes rock.

Erosion of Rock by Ice

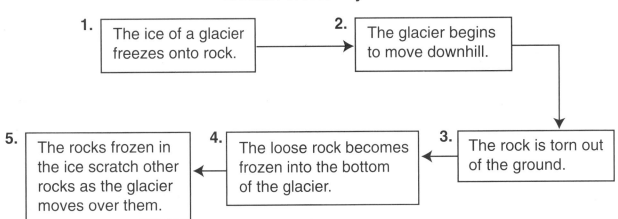

1. The ice of a glacier freezes onto rock.
2. The glacier begins to move downhill.
3. The rock is torn out of the ground.
4. The loose rock becomes frozen into the bottom of the glacier.
5. The rocks frozen in the ice scratch other rocks as the glacier moves over them.

A flowchart can help you see how a fossil is formed in sedimentary rock. **Complete the following flowchart to show the sequence of events.** Two of the boxes have already been filled for you.

Steps in the Formation of a Fossil

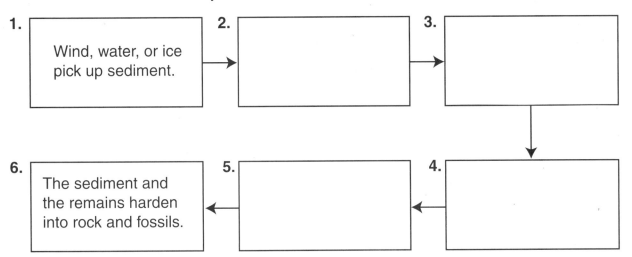

1. Wind, water, or ice pick up sediment.
2.
3.
4.
5.
6. The sediment and the remains harden into rock and fossils.

© Macmillan/McGraw-Hill

Sequence of Events

Life is a series of sequences, such as eating dinner, getting dressed, taking a trip, playing baseball, and going to bed. Sometimes you have to decide what you can do based on sequence. Look at the camp schedule below. It lists activities and the times they are available. **Use information from the schedule to answer the questions and make your own sequence of events.**

Camp Lotsafun Schedule

8:00 A.M. All campers arrive by bus.

8:30 A.M.-12:30 P.M. Activities

12:30-1:00 P.M. Lunch is available.

1:00-1:30 P.M. Lunch is available.

1:30-4:00 P.M. Activities

4:15 P.M. Buses leave.

Acting

9:00-10:00 A.M.

11:00 A.M.-noon

12:30-1:30 P.M.

1:30-2:30 P.M.

3:00-4:00 P.M.

Boating

9:00-10:30 A.M.

11:00 A.M.-12:30 P.M.

2:00 A.M.-3:30 P.M.

Crafts

8:30-9:30 A.M.

10:30-11:30 A.M.

1:30-2:30 P.M.

2:30-3:30 P.M.

Gymnastics

8:30-9:00 A.M.

10:00-10:30 A.M.

noon-12:30 P.M.

1:30-2:00 P.M.

3:00-3:30 P.M.

Horseback Riding

9:00-10:00 A.M.

10:00-11:00 A.M.

11:30-12:30 P.M.

1:00-2:00 P.M.

2:00-3:00 P.M.

3:00-4:00 P.M.

Soccer

9:00-11:30 A.M.

11:00 A.M.-1:00 P.M.

2:00-4:00 P.M.

1. What time do you get to camp? _____

2. What time do you go home? _____

3. When is lunch available? _____

4. Make a schedule that allows you to take acting, gymnastics, and boating *or* horseback riding, crafts, and soccer and still have lunch!

©Macmillan/McGraw-Hill

One Step at a Time

We do everything in sequence, one step at a time. First you use dishes, then you wash them, dry them, and put them away. When you get a glass of milk or spend a day in school, you follow a step-by-step sequence.

Number the entries on each list below to show the sequence of events. Add entries if you want flavored milk or do other things at school.

Get a Glass of Milk	My Day at School
_____ Drink the milk. Yum!	_____ Go home from school.
_____ Dry the glass.	_____ Have gym class.
_____ Pour the milk.	_____ Have math class.
_____ Put the glass away.	_____ Arrive at school.
_____ Get milk from the refrigerator.	_____ Have science class.
_____ Wash out the glass.	_____ Have lunch.
_____ Put milk back in the refrigerator.	_____ Have social studies class.
_____ Get a drinking glass.	_____ Hand in homework.

Now write the step-by-step sequence to explain where rocks eroded by either wind, moving ice, or water go, using page C25 in your book.

_____

_____

_____

_____

_____

©Macmillan/McGraw-Hill

Earth and Its Neighbors

Fill in the blanks. Reading Skill: **Sequence of Events** - questions 4, 5, 16

What Is the Solar System?

1. The _____ is the Sun and the objects traveling around it.

2. The objects around the Sun include nine _____.

3. The path of a planet is called its _____.

4. Earth is the _____ planet from the Sun.

5. A complete trip of Earth around the Sun takes one _____.

What Keeps the Planets in Orbit?

6. The force of attraction between the Sun and Earth
is called _____.

7. Gravity depends on two measurements: _____.

8. The closer two objects are, the _____ the pull of
gravity between them.

9. Newton's ideas are called the law of _____ gravitation.

10. The planets are kept in orbit by the Sun's _____.

11. The tendency of a moving object to keep moving in a straight
line is called _____.

12. Both _____ and _____ keep the
planets in their orbits.

What Makes a Day?

13. All planets spin, or _____, like huge spinning tops.

14. How much light and warmth a planet receives depends on _____.

15. The length of a day on Earth is _____.

What Causes Earth's Seasons?

16. As the third planet from the Sun, Earth is at a location where it receives just the right amount of _____ to provide living things with the warmth and light they need.

17. Earth's orbit is a slightly stretched circle, or _____.

18. Colder winters and warmer summers are caused by Earth's _____.

What Is Planet Earth Like?

19. The hard, outer layer of Earth is the _____.

20. The rocky surface that makes up the top of the lithosphere is the _____.

21. The crust has the soil and many other _____.

22. The _____ also includes Earth's lakes, rivers, streams, underground water, and ice besides the ocean.

23. The hydrosphere acts as a big _____.

What Is the Moon Like?

24. The Moon has no hydrosphere; there is no _____ to drink; there is no _____.

What Are Constellations?

25. In the past, people looked at the stars and saw them arranged in groups that formed patterns in the sky; they called these patterns _____.

© Macmillan/McGraw-Hill

What Keeps the Planets in Orbit?

This diagram has three arrows to show three different possible paths that Earth could take. The solid arrow shows Earth's actual path. The dashed arrows show what would happen if only gravity or inertia acted on Earth. Compare the three paths.

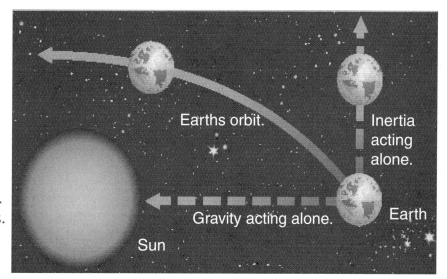

Earths orbit.

Inertia acting alone.

Gravity acting alone.

Earth

Sun

Answer these questions about the diagram above.

1. What would happen if only gravity were operating on Earth?

   _____

2. Would this path take Earth closer to the Sun or farther away from the Sun?

   _____

3. What would happen if only inertia were acting on Earth?

   _____

4. Would this path take Earth closer to the Sun or farther away from the Sun?

   _____

5. Why does Earth's path bend around the Sun?

   _____

   _____

6. What do you think would happen if Earth were not moving?

   _____

What Causes Earth's Seasons?

Diagrams like this one explain what is happening at different seasons. It shows how Earth changes as it revolves around the Sun. The arrows show the direction of Earth's path. By following the arrows from globe to globe you can follow how Earth changes its tilt toward the Sun. Make sure you understand what is happening to the Earth at each time of the year.

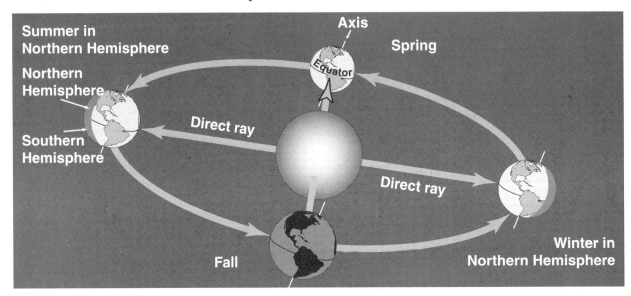

Answer these questions about the diagram above.

1. Which hemisphere is tilted toward the Sun when it is winter in the Northern Hemisphere? _____

2. What season is it in the Northern Hemisphere when this hemisphere is tilted toward the Sun? _____

3. What do you think happens to the Northern Hemisphere between summer and winter? _____

_____

4. What do you think direct rays have to do with the fact that summer is warmer than winter? _____

_____

5. Look closely at one of the illustrations of Earth. Why is a line shown going through Earth? _____

_____

Earth and Its Neighbors

Match the correct letter with the description.

_____ 1. the hard, outer layer of Earth

_____ 2. a force of attraction between any object and any other objects around it

_____ 3. any material that helps support life on Earth

_____ 4. groups of stars that form patterns in the sky

_____ 5. the Sun and the objects that are traveling around it

_____ 6. the third planet from the Sun

_____ 7. the rocky surface that makes up the top of the lithosphere

_____ 8. Earth's water

_____ 9. any of the nine objects that travel around the Sun

_____ 10. the tendency of a moving object to keep moving in a straight line

_____ 11. layers of gases that surround Earth

Vocabulary

a. solar system
b. planet
c. gravity
d. inertia
e. lithosphere
f. crust
g. resource
h. hydrosphere
i. atmosphere
j. Earth
k. constellations

Fill in the blanks to describe how the Sun affects Earth.

12. The Sun holds Earth in orbit because of _____ and _____.

13. The Sun also provides Earth with _____ and _____.

14. The Sun's light shines more or less directly on parts of Earth because of Earth's _____.

Earth and Its Neighbors

Vocabulary

rotates	system	orbit	third
reflect	24	gravity	mass

Fill in the blanks.

The Sun and the objects that travel around it form the solar

_____. Each planet travels in a path called a(n)

_____. These planets don't give off light; instead they

_____ sunlight. Each planet spins, or _____,

making a complete turn during its day. For Earth, this day-night cycle takes

_____ hours. Earth is the _____ planet

from the Sun. An invisible force called _____ keeps Earth

from flying off into space. This force of attraction depends on distance

and _____.

Earth's Changing Crust

Fill in the blanks. Reading Skill: **Sequence of Events** - questions 6, 7, 13, 14, 17, 21, 22

What Makes the Crust Move?

1. Cracks in Earth's crust are called _____.

2. Devices called _____ record the motions of Earth's crust.

3. Surveyors leave _____ that tell the exact elevation of a place.

4. Scientists who study Earth are called _____.

5. The crust is only _____ of Earth's thickness.

6. Under the crust is the _____, Earth's thickest layer.

7. Below the mantle is Earth's _____, with liquid and solid parts.

8. Pieces of Earth's crust that move along the surface are called _____.

What Forces Act on the Crust?

9. The force that stretches or pulls apart the crust is _____.

10. The force that squeezes or pushes the crust together is _____.

11. The force that twists, tears, or pushes one part of the crust past another is _____.

12. Mountains made of crumpled and folded layers of rock are called _____.

© Macmillan/McGraw-Hill

13. Hot, molten rock deep below Earth's surface is _____; when it comes to the surface it is _____.

14. Blocks of crust moving along a fault can form _____ _____.

What Other Forces Shape Earth's Surface?

15. The breaking down of materials of Earth's crust into smaller pieces is _____.

16. The picking up and carrying away of the pieces is called _____.

17. Changes in temperature cause rock to _____ and _____.

How Can Wind and Ice Erode Rock?

18. Wind mostly erodes pieces of rock that are the size of _____ particles or smaller.

19. A moving river of ice that carries rocks and wears away the land is called a _____.

Where Do Eroded Rocks Go?

20. The dropping off of bits of eroded rock is called _____.

21. Deposition can gradually fill up depressions, or _____, in Earth's surface.

What Forces Shape the Moon's Surface?

22. The only weathering and erosion on the Moon is caused by _____ that strike its surface.

© Macmillan/McGraw-Hill

What Makes the Crust Move?

A cross section shows what is inside something. Some cross sections, like this one, show not only what is inside but also what the parts are doing. In this diagram, you should be able to pick out the parts of Earth as well as words that show motion.

Layers of Earth

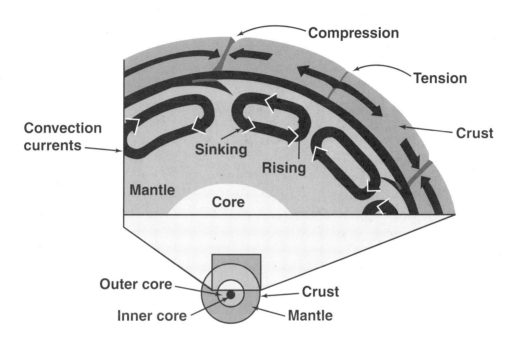

Answer these questions about the diagram above.

1. What three parts of Earth are shown in the diagram?

_____

2. What words of motion can you find?

_____

3. What is happening during compression?

_____

4. How would you describe tension?

_____

5. What happens in a convection current?

_____

©Macmillan/McGraw-Hill

What Forces Act on the Crust?

Diagrams like this one show how forces act. This diagram shows three forces that act on Earth's crust. The arrows tell you the direction in which each force acts and how the force makes the rock layers move.

FORCES IN THE CRUST

Tension

Compression   Shear

Answer these questions about the diagram above.

1. What three forces are shown in the diagram?

_____

2. Which forces act mostly in a horizontal direction?

_____

3. Which force acts mostly in a vertical direction? _____

4. What results from tension between rock layers?

_____

5. What happens when a shear force acts on rock layers?

_____

6. What does compression do to rock layers?

_____

7. Which forces do you think could cause mountains to form?

_____

©Macmillan/McGraw-Hill

Earth's Changing Crust

Match the correct letter with the description.

_____ 1. magma that reaches Earth's surface

_____ 2. the dropping off of bits of eroded rock

_____ 3. a crack in the crust, whose sides show evidence of motion

_____ 4. the picking up and carrying away of pieces of rock

_____ 5. someone who measures Earth's elevation and leaves plaques called bench marks

_____ 6. a scientist who studies Earth

_____ 7. a delicate device that records the motion of Earth's crust

_____ 8. hot, molten rock deep below Earth's surface

_____ 9. a chunk of rock from space that strikes a surface, such as Earth

_____ 10. the breaking down of rocks into smaller pieces

Vocabulary

a. fault

b. geologist

c. magma

d. lava

e. weathering

f. erosion

g. deposition

h. meteorite

i. seismograph

j. surveyor

Fill in the correct term.

11. stretches or pulls apart the crust: _____

12. twists, tears, or pushes one part of the crust past another: _____

13. squeezes or pushes the crust together: _____

14. mountains made of crumpled and folded layers of rock: _____

15. mountains formed by blocks of crust moving along a fault: _____

© Macmillan/McGraw-Hill

Earth's Changing Crust

Vocabulary

geologists	crack	seismographs	marks
sea	California	vibrations	predict

Fill in the blanks.

Earthquakes commonly occur where Earth has a fault or

_____ in its crust. One big fault runs through most of the

state of _____. During an earthquake, _____

travel through the crust. This motion can be recorded by devices named

_____. Surveyors measure elevation or how high a location

is above _____ level. They use plaques called bench

_____ to detect crust movement. Scientists who study Earth

are _____. They try to _____ an earthquake

by recording tiny movements.

©Macmillan/McGraw-Hill

Minerals of Earth's Crust

Fill in the blanks. Reading Skill: **Sequence of Events** - question 5, 11, 13, 14

How Can You Identify a Mineral?

1. Solid materials of Earth's crust are called _____.

2. Like all matter, minerals are made of _____.

3. Most minerals are chemical _____, that is, two or more elements joined together.

4. Minerals form geometric shapes, called _____.

5. You should always observe _____ on a fresh surface.

6. The way light bounces off a mineral is called _____.

How Else Can You Identify Minerals?

7. The color of the powder left when a mineral is rubbed against a hard, rough surface is called its _____.

8. The measure of how well a mineral resists scratching is called its _____.

9. If a mineral breaks along flat surfaces, it is called _____.

10. Minerals that do not break smoothly are said to have _____.

How Do Minerals Form?

11. Many rocks form when hot liquid rock, or _____, cools.

12. Some of the rarest minerals, like _____, form deep within Earth.

13. Cooling hot water can form _____ that settle to the bottom of the water.

14. Common table salt is formed when ocean water _____.

What Are Minerals Used For?

15. A mineral that contains a useful substance is called a(n) _____.

16. Iron comes from the mineral _____.

17. Substances that conduct electricity and can be stretched into wires are _____.

18. Minerals valued for being rare and beautiful are called _____.

How Can You Identify a Mineral?

These pictures illustrate six minerals of Earth's crust. The diagrams show that each mineral forms a different geometric shape. To compare the diagrams of the shapes, look at the lengths of the sides of each crystal. Also notice the angles at which those sides meet.

The mineral chalcopyrite (kal·kuh·PIGH·right) is a compound made of the elements copper, iron, and sulfur. It is where much of our copper comes from. Copper is used for wire, coins, pots, and pans.

Tetragonal crystal

Triclinic crystal

The mineral kaolinite (KAY·uh·luh·night) is used in china plates and ceramic objects. It comes in many colors—red, white, reddish brown, and even black.

Rock salt, which is used to melt ice, is the mineral halite (HAL·ight). It is a compound made of the elements sodium and chlorine.

Cubic crystal

Monoclinic crystal

The "lead" in a lead pencil is not the metal element lead at all. It is the mineral graphite (GRAF·ight), which is a form of the element carbon.

Hexagonal crystal

Topaz is a mineral used in many kinds of jewelry. It comes in many colors— pink, pale blue, and even yellow or white.

Orthorhombic crystal

Talc is the mineral used in talcum powder. Talc comes in white and greenish colors.

Answer these questions about the diagram above.

1. From what mineral do we get most of our copper? _____

2. What is graphite? _____

3. What is rock salt? _____

4. What is topaz? _____

5. Which crystals have sides that tilt? _____

6. Which crystal has the most sides? _____

7. What is one difference between a tetragonal crystal and a cubic crystal?

_____

How Else Can You Identify Minerals?

This table shows calcite and its properties. Read about each of the properties of calcite.

MINERAL	COLOR(S)	LUSTER (Shiny as Metals)	PORCELAIN PLATE TEST (Streak)	CLEAVAGE (Number)	HARDNESS (Tools scratched by)	DENSITY (Compared with water)
Calcite	colorless, white, pale blue	no	colorless, white	yes—3	3 (all but fingernail)	2.7

Answer these questions about the table above.

1. Why is the color of calcite listed as colorless, white, or pale blue?

_____

2. What does it mean that calcite has no luster?

_____

3. What would be a good title for this table?

_____

4. How would you test for hardness?

_____

_____

_____

5. What does a density of 2.7 mean?

_____

Minerals of Earth's Crust

You are given an unknown mineral. How would you identify it?
Fill in the table below.

Property	Definition	How Accurate Is It? Explain.
color	1.	2.
luster	3.	4.
hardness	5.	6.
streak	7.	8.
cleavage	9.	10.

Give an example of each and describe a property.

11. crystals _____

12. ores _____

13. gems _____

14. metals _____

Answer the questions.

15. Define mineral and describe why minerals are a nonrenewable resource.

_____

_____

Minerals of Earth's Crust

Vocabulary

plate	luster	fracture	cleavage
color	scratching	metallic	diamond

Fill in the blanks.

You can identify minerals by the _____ or way the light

bounces off their surfaces. Minerals with a(n) _____

luster are shiny. Another way to tell minerals apart is by observing

_____ on a fresh surface. You can tell gold from pyrite by

using a streak _____. Hardness, or how well a mineral

resists _____, is measured by Mohs' scale. The hardest

mineral is a(n) _____. If a mineral has _____,

it will break along flat surfaces. If it has _____, it wouldn't

break smoothly.

Earth's Rocks and Soil

Fill in the blanks. Reading Skill: **Sequence of Events** - questions 3, 4, 8, 10, 11

How Are Rocks Alike and Different?

1. A _____ is any naturally formed solid in the crust made up of one or more kinds of minerals.

What Are Igneous Rocks?

2. Rocks that form when melted rock material cools and hardens are called _____ rocks.

What Are Sedimentary Rocks?

3. Small bits of matter joined together form _____ rock.

How Are Sedimentary Rocks Useful?

4. Sandstone and limestone are both used to make _____.

5. Sedimentary rocks sometimes contain _____, or the remains or imprints of living things of the past.

What Are Metamorphic Rocks?

6. When a rock is heated to high temperatures at great depth, the minerals change in some way and form _____ rock.

How Are Metamorphic Rocks Used?

7. A useful "rock makeover" that contains minerals with brilliant colors and is easy to carve is _____.

Where Does Soil Come From?

8. The main ingredient in soil is weathered _____.

9. Decayed plant and animal material in soil is called _____.

How Can People Ruin Soil?

10. People bury garbage and _____ in soil and spray _____ on soil to kill pests.

11. People also throw foam cups and plastic materials on the ground, which contributes to _____.

How Can People Protect the Soil?

12. People can add materials called _____ and humus to replace minerals removed by crops.

13. Farmers can plow furrows across a slope rather than up and down, which is called _____.

What Is the Rock Cycle?

14. The never-ending series of processes by which rocks change from one form to another is called the _____.

©Macmillan/McGraw-Hill

How Are Metamorphic Rocks Used?

This diagram shows how coal is formed. Notice that above the drawings there is a bar that tells how long ago each step took place. The oldest stage is at the left, and the present stage is shown at the right.

Millions of Years Ago

300	280	220	150	10	Present
A forest swamp	Plants die and sink to the bottom.	A thick layer of peat, partly decayed plants, builds up.	The swamp dries up. Buried under layers of sediment, the peat changes to a sedimentary rock called lignite (LIG·night).	Buried by more and more layers of sediment, the lignite becomes more compacted. It forms bituminous coal.	Buried even deeper, bituminous coal is changed by great heat and pressure. It forms anthracite, a metamorphic rock.

Peat   **Lignite**   **Bituminous (soft) coal (sedimentary rock)**   **Anthracite (hard) coal (metamorphic rock)**

Answer these question about the diagram above.

1. Where does coal come from? _____

2. What is peat? _____

3. What does peat change into? _____

4. What happens to the lignite? _____

_____

5. What does lignite become? _____

6. How is bituminous coal changed to anthracite coal? _____

_____

7. What kind of rock is anthracite coal? _____

©Macmillan/McGraw-Hill

Where Does Soil Come From?

This cross section shows what you would see if you could slice through Earth's crust. You would see layers, or horizons, of soil. The arrows point to the top and bottom of each of the three horizons, and to the top of the bedrock layer.

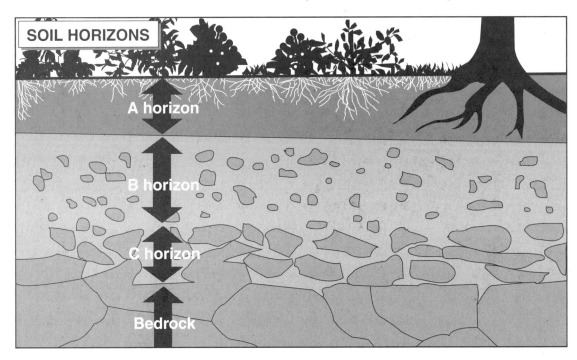

Answer these questions about the diagram above.

1. What would you expect to find in the A horizon?

   _____

2. What is in the B horizon? _____

3. How do the rocks of the C horizon differ from those in the B horizon?

   _____

4. Into which layer or layers do the roots of most plants reach? _____

5. How do you think the bedrock got its name?

   _____

6. Which rocks do you think are most like the bedrock? Why? _____

   _____

Earth's Rocks and Soil

Match the correct letter with the description.

_____ 1. rocks changing from one form into another in a never-ending series of processes

_____ 2. decayed plant or animal material in soil

_____ 3. any remains or imprint of living things of the past

_____ 4. a naturally formed solid in the crust, made up of one or more minerals

_____ 5. adding any harmful substances to Earth's land, water, or air

_____ 6. a rock formed from another kind of rock under heat and pressure

_____ 7. a rock made of bits of matter joined together

_____ 8. a rock formed when melted rock material cools and hardens

Vocabulary

a. rock

b. fossil

c. humus

d. pollution

e. rock cycle

f. igneous rock

g. sedimentary rock

h. metamorphic rock

Answer the question.

9. What does soil have to do with rocks?

_____

_____

Earth's Rocks and Soil

Vocabulary

chemicals	nutrients	wastes	forest
pollution	decay	graze	erosion

Fill in the blanks.

People ruin soil by burying hazardous _____ and garbage in it. They spray soil with _____ to kill weeds. These materials add up to _____ which is adding any harmful substance to Earth's land, water, or air. Trash like plastic that doesn't _____ makes soil unusable. When people grow the same crops every year, it depletes the _____ in soil. If plants are removed, wind and rain will expose soil to _____. Another cause is allowing cattle to _____ too long in the same spot. The soil is exposed whenever a(n) _____ is cut down.

Rocks and Minerals

Circle the letter of the best answer.

1. The nine objects that travel around the Sun and reflect its light are
   a. meteorites.
   b. moons.
   c. planets.
   d. solar systems.

2. The tendency of a moving object to keep moving in a straight line is called
   a. gravity.
   b. inertia.
   c. rotation.
   d. tilt.

3. Earth's water is called the
   a. atmosphere.
   b. crust.
   c. hydrosphere.
   d. lithosphere.

4. The rocky surface that makes up the top of the lithosphere is Earth's
   a. crust.
   b. hydrosphere.
   c. rock cycle.
   d. soil horizon.

5. Any material that helps support life on Earth is called a(n)
   a. gem.
   b. mineral.
   c. ore.
   d. resource.

6. A crack in Earth's crust with sides that show evidence of motion is a(n)
   a. cleavage.
   b. deposition.
   c. fault.
   d. shear.

7. A scientist who studies Earth is called a(n)
   a. geologist.
   b. astronomer.
   c. mineralogist.
   d. gemologist.

Circle the letter of the best answer.

8. Hot, molten rock deep below Earth's surface is

   a. deposition.   b. humus.

   c. lava.   d. magma.

9. The breaking down of rocks into smaller pieces is called

   a. deposition.   b. erosion.

   c. pollution.   d. weathering.

10. A chunk of rock from space that strikes Earth is a(n)

    a. gem.   b. meteorite.

    c. mineral.   d. ore.

11. A solid material of Earth's crust with a definite composition is a(n)

    a. fossil.   b. mineral.

    c. volcano.   d. meteorite.

12. How well a mineral resists scratching is called its

    a. cleavage.   b. hardness.

    c. luster.   d. streak.

13. A rock formed when melted rock material cools and hardens is

    a. humus.   b. igneous.

    c. metamorphic.   d. sedimentary.

14. Any remains or imprint of living things of the past describes a(n)

    a. fossil.   b. gem.

    c. ore.   d. rock.

Chapter Summary

1. What is the name of the chapter you just finished reading?

   _____

   _____

2. What are four vocabulary words you learned in the chapter?
   Write a definition for each.

   _____

   _____

   _____

   _____

   _____

   _____

   _____

   _____

3. What are two main ideas that you learned in this chapter?

   _____

   _____

   _____

   _____

   _____

   _____

©Macmillan/McGraw-Hill

Air, Water, and Energy

Each energy source listed in the word bank below is either a fossil fuel or an alternative energy source. Also, each energy source is either a renewable resource or a nonrenewable resource. Write each energy source in the correct box at the bottom of the page. After you have classified each energy source, underline any that pollute the environment and circle any that come from biomass.

For example, propane is a fossil fuel. It is also a nonrenewable source of energy. Propane has been written in the correct box. It is not underlined or circled, because it does not come from biomass, and it does not pollute the environment when it is burned.

Word Bank		
animal wastes	coal	falling water
gasoline	geothermal energy	natural gas
oil	plant matter	propane
sunlight	wind	wood

	Renewable Resource	Nonrenewable Resource
Fossil Fuel		propane
Alternative Energy Source		

©Macmillan/McGraw-Hill

Draw Conclusions

Read each description. Then draw and label your conclusion of what it is.

Water goes around with me! I mean, I renew, or recycle, it so you can have fresh water to drink. What am I? _____	The wind spins my "arms" around. That energy runs generators that make electricity. What am I? _____
I carry energy from place to place. Each water particle in me moves in a circle. When I break I can be very powerful. What am I? _____	People say I hang like a brown cloud over many cities. I'm a mixture of smoke and fog. What am I? _____

T

Check the Facts

Remember, you can't draw a conclusion unless you have all the facts. Read each set of facts below. Can you draw a conclusion? If not, circle **not enough facts.** If you can, circle your answer.

1. Fossil fuels formed as the remains of ancient plants and animals decayed. Dinosaurs were ancient animals. Are some fossil fuels formed from the decayed remains of dinosaurs?

   yes   no   **not enough facts**

2. Wastes from burning fossil fuels go into the air. They can mix with moisture to produce acid rain. Should people stop burning fossil fuels forever?

   yes   no   **not enough facts**

3. Steve's father was a football star for his high school and for his college. Steve plans to go to the same high school and college his dad did. Will Steve be a football star in those schools?

   yes   no   **not enough facts**

4. The fifth graders at Sloane School started a recycling program. The kids have also looked for ways to save electricity in the school and in their homes. Next Saturday they plan to clean up a nearby park and plant some flowers and shrubs. Do the fifth graders care about our environment?

   yes   no   not enough facts

5. Kyle is shorter than Mark but taller than Alex. Alex is shorter than Rudy. Is Rudy taller than Kyle?

   yes   **no**   **not enough facts**

6. Marta got a 94 on the test. Luis and Diane got 92. Danny, Jackie, and Allie got 90, and Roger had 89. The other kids had lower scores. Did Marta do better on the test than the other kids?

   yes   no   not enough facts

Earth's Atmosphere

Fill in the blanks. 📖 Reading Skill: **Draw Conclusions** - question 7

Why Do Living Things Need the Atmosphere?

1. Air is a mixture of nitrogen, _____, and water vapor.

2. On land, living things have structures that enable them to get _____ directly from air.

3. Oxygen helps provide us with energy by breaking down _____.

4. After food is broken down, living things give off the gas _____.

5. The gas that is given off by animals is used by _____ to make food.

6. The process by which plants make food and give off oxygen is called _____.

7. Oxygen is called a(n) _____ resource because it can be replaced.

8. The _____ protects us from the Sun's harmful ultraviolet rays.

9. The atmosphere also protects us from rocks from space. The _____ with the air burns them up before they can come to Earth.

10. Clouds in the atmosphere help regulate_____.

11. About 78 percent of the air is _____, which is an important part of proteins.

What Causes Pollution?

12. Many pollutants get into the air from burning _____.

13. These fuels were formed from the decay of ancient _____.

14. Fossil fuels are _____ resources.

15. Other fossil fuels include _____, _____, and _____.

16. Even plowing farm fields can cause air pollution by adding _____ to the atmosphere.

17. Natural events like _____ and _____ can add particles and smoke to the air.

18. Many cities experience _____, a mixture of smoke and fog.

19. At ground level, the gas _____ can make people sick.

What Is Acid Rain?

20. Burning fossil fuels can cause harmful chemicals called acids to form in the atmosphere, which then fall to Earth in the form of _____.

How Can We Clean Up the Air?

21. The United States passed the _____ in 1967 to decrease air pollution.

22. To protect the air, we can limit the amount of _____ in refrigerators and air conditioners.

Why Do Living Things Need the Atmosphere?

This diagram shows the carbon dioxide-oxygen cycle. Notice how the flow is circular. By following the arrows you can see how carbon dioxide and oxygen circulate through the atmosphere.

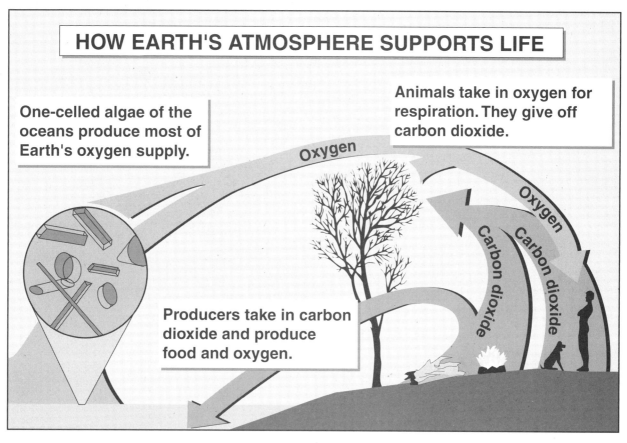

HOW EARTH'S ATMOSPHERE SUPPORTS LIFE

One-celled algae of the oceans produce most of Earth's oxygen supply.

Animals take in oxygen for respiration. They give off carbon dioxide.

Oxygen

Oxygen

Carbon dioxide

Carbon dioxide

Producers take in carbon dioxide and produce food and oxygen.

Answer these questions about the diagram above.

1. What role do trees play in the carbon dioxide-oxygen cycle?

_____

2. What organisms produce most of Earth's oxygen supply?

_____

3. What role do animals and humans play in this cycle?

_____

4. What do producers produce besides oxygen? _____

How the Atmosphere Supports Life

The pictures below shows two ways that the atmosphere helps to protect life on Earth. The first picture shows how nitrogen is cycled. The second picture shows how convection currents circulate air temperatures.

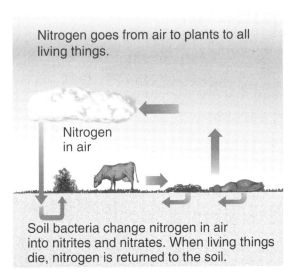

Nitrogen goes from air to plants to all living things.

Nitrogen in air

Soil bacteria change nitrogen in air into nitrites and nitrates. When living things die, nitrogen is returned to the soil.

Air circulates in patterns called convection currents.

Warm air rising

Cold air sinking

Answer the following questions about the pictures above.

1. What kind of currents are caused by warm air rising and cold air sinking?

   _____

   _____

2. When is nitrogen returned to the soil?

   _____

   _____

3. What do soil bacteria do?

   _____

   _____

©Macmillan/McGraw-Hill

Earth's Atmosphere

Match the correct letter with the description.

_____ 1. a mixture of smoke and fog

_____ 2. a resource that can be replaced in a short period of time

_____ 3. a resource that cannot be replaced in your lifetime

_____ 4. a fuel formed from the decay of ancient forms of life

_____ 5. moisture that falls to Earth after being mixed with wastes from burned fossil fuels

_____ 6. the part of the atmosphere that screens out much of the Sun's UV rays

Vocabulary

a. renewable resource

b. ozone layer

c. fossil fuel

d. smog

e. acid rain

f. nonrenewable resource

Write a one-sentence summary to answer each of these questions.

7. How do animals use oxygen? _____

8. How does the atmosphere protect living things? _____

9. What makes air dirty? _____

10. How can rain be harmful? _____

11. How can we clean up the air? _____

12. How does smog affect you? _____

©Macmillan/McGraw-Hill

Earth's Atmosphere

Vocabulary

ozone	fossil fuels	CFCs	breathing
fires	smog	radiation	

Fill in the blanks.

Many pollutants get into the air from burning _____.

Natural events such as grass and forest _____ spread

smoke. A mixture of smoke and fog known as _____

hangs over many cities like a brown cloud. It can kill people who have

_____ problems. There are holes in the _____

layer. These allow harmful UV _____ through. Substances

called _____ are released from products like refrigerators

and aerosol spray cans. They rise into the atmosphere where they can affect

the ozone layer.

Earth's Fresh Water

Fill in the blanks. Reading Skill: **Draw Conclusions** - questions 5, 7, 9, 11, 15

How Do We Use Earth's Oceans?

1. The oceans provide us with food we call _____ and minerals.

2. Nodules, or lumps, of _____ can be picked up from the sea floor.

3. Offshore rigs pump _____ and natural gas from beneath the ocean floor.

4. The process by which we get fresh water from seawater is called _____.

5. Water leaves dissolved materials behind when it _____.

Where Is Fresh Water From?

6. Fresh water is constantly renewed in the _____.

7. Water is on the move–as a liquid that changes to a _____ and then back to a _____.

8. The main source of water in the water cycle is the _____.

9. The main sources of fresh water on land are _____ and _____, which fall as _____.

10. Plants give off _____.

11. The water that seeps into the spaces between bits of rock and soil is called _____.

12. The top of the water-filled spaces is called the _____.

13. An underground layer of rock or soil that is filled with water is called a(n) _____.

14. Some groundwater seeps out of the ground in a(n) _____.

15. A hole dug below the water table so water can be brought up for drinking is called a(n) _____.

How Can Fresh Water Be Polluted?

16. Rain and snow can pick up pollutants in the _____.

17. Runoff water can carry pollutants from _____ into streams or lakes.

18. As water soaks down through the soil, it can pick up chemicals called _____.

How Can We Purify Water?

19. The ground acts as a fine screen to trap, or _____, dirt particles in water.

20. In water purification plants, water is filtered by _____.

21. To kill bacteria, _____ is added to water.

Where Is Fresh Water From?

This diagram shows the water cycle, a giant circle in which water moves around Earth and the atmosphere. Follow the circle from number 1 to number 5. Also notice the arrows that show the movement of water into and through Earth.

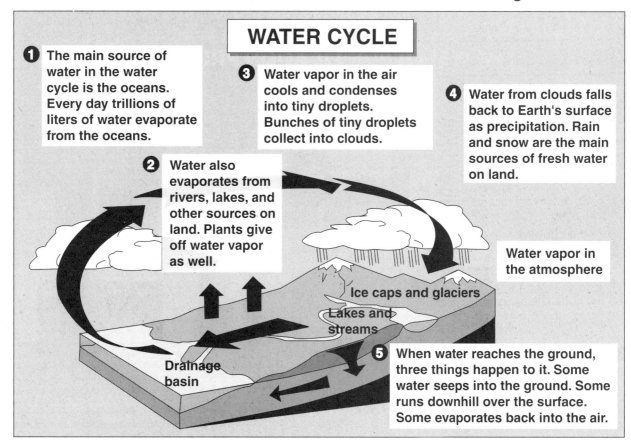

WATER CYCLE

1 The main source of water in the water cycle is the oceans. Every day trillions of liters of water evaporate from the oceans.

2 Water also evaporates from rivers, lakes, and other sources on land. Plants give off water vapor as well.

3 Water vapor in the air cools and condenses into tiny droplets. Bunches of tiny droplets collect into clouds.

4 Water from clouds falls back to Earth's surface as precipitation. Rain and snow are the main sources of fresh water on land.

Water vapor in the atmosphere

Ice caps and glaciers

Lakes and streams

Drainage basin

5 When water reaches the ground, three things happen to it. Some water seeps into the ground. Some runs downhill over the surface. Some evaporates back into the air.

Answer these questions about the diagram above.

1. Where does most of the water in the water cycle come from? _____

2. What are other sources of water? _____

3. How are rain droplets formed? _____

4. What are the main sources of fresh water on land? _____

5. What happens after water reaches the ground? _____

_____

_____

6. What process moves water into the air? _____

7. What process brings water down to Earth? _____

How Can We Purify Water?

This diagram shows how water is purified so we can drink it. Although individual water purification plants vary, the basic elements are the same. Follow the arrows to see the direction in which water moves through the process. Identify each step and read the paragraphs to learn about the process.

THE WATER PURIFICATION PROCESS

1 Water is often treated with chemicals that make particles in the water clump together. The big particles then sink to the bottom.

4 Chlorine is added to kill bacteria. Many cities also add fluoride, which helps prevent cavities in your teeth.

Pumps

Settling basin

Offices

Factories

Homes

Raw water

Mixing basin

Pumps

2 Then the water flows through layers of gravel and fine sand. The gravel and sand filter out smaller particles from the water.

3 Air may be bubbled through the water to improve the taste.

Answer these questions about the diagram above.

1. What do chemicals do to water at the beginning of the purification process?

_____

_____

2. What do fine sand and gravel do to the water?

_____

3. What is used to improve the taste of water? _____

4. What chemical is added to kill bacteria? _____

5. How do you benefit when fluoride is added to drinking water?

_____

6. What is used to move the water along during the purification process? _____

_____

©Macmillan/McGraw-Hill

Earth's Fresh Water

Match the correct letter with the description.

_____ 1. from this we get seafood, minerals, and fossil fuels

_____ 2. water that seeps into the ground into spaces between bits of rock and soil

_____ 3. a place where groundwater seeps out of the ground

_____ 4. the continuous movement of water between Earth's surface and the air; it helps clean water

_____ 5. an underground layer of rock or soil filled with water

_____ 6. a storage area for freshwater supplies

_____ 7. a hole dug below the water table that water seeps into

_____ 8. getting freshwater from seawater

_____ 9. most of Earth's water is this type

_____ 10. the top of the water-filled spaces in the ground

Vocabulary

a. desalination
b. water cycle
c. groundwater
d. water table
e. aquifer
f. spring
g. well
h. reservoir
i. salt water
j. ocean

Write "ocean water" or "freshwater" to identify if these things are more likely to pollute ocean water or freshwater.

11. water traveling over garbage _____

12. a barge going out to dump wastes _____

13. acid rain _____

14. spills from oil tankers _____

15. pesticides _____

© Macmillan/McGraw-Hill

Earth's Fresh Water

Vocabulary

desalination	wells	spring	seawater
reservoirs	pipelines	table	aquifers

Fill in the blanks.

You can't use _____ to drink or sprinkle plants. A process called _____ allows you to obtain freshwater from oceans. People in cities get water from _____, storage areas for freshwater. This water is transported by _____ to locations where it's needed. Some people tap into groundwater by digging _____. These holes are dug beneath the water _____. Other holes are dug into _____ sandwiched between rock layers. Some groundwater seeps out in a place called a(n) _____.

Earth's Oceans

Fill in the blanks. 📖 Reading Skill: **Draw Conclusions** - questions 1, 3, 4, 6, 10, 12, 16

What Are Oceans, Seas, and Basins?

1. Most of Earth's water is contained in large bodies of salt water called _____.

2. The ocean floor, or _____, contains mountains, valleys, and plains.

3. If all the water evaporated from the oceans, a layer of _____ about 60 meters (200 feet) thick would be left on the ocean floor.

4. When volcanoes erupt, they let out water _____ and other gases.

5. Seawater is an important source of _____.

6. Drilling rigs are used to extract _____ and _____ from the land beneath the sea.

What Causes Ocean Currents?

7. A stream of water that flows through the ocean like a river is a _____.

8. _____ currents are driven by the wind.

How Does the Water in a Wave Move?

9. As a wave passes through the ocean, water _____ move in circles.

10. Each _____ may hurl thousands of tons of water against the shore, breaking rocks apart and smoothing the fragments into pebbles and sand.

©Macmillan/McGraw-Hill

What Causes the Tides?

11. The pull of the Moon and Sun's gravity on Earth causes _____.

12. The combined pull of the Sun and the Moon during times of New and Full Moons causes the highest high tides and lowest low tides, called _____ tides.

13. _____ tides have the smallest range.

What Is the Ocean Floor Like?

14. The underwater edge of a continent is called its _____.

15. The _____ leads steeply down from the continental shelf toward the sea floor.

16. The _____ is a buildup of sediment on the sea floor at the bottom of the continental slope.

17. One of the flattest places on Earth, the _____ plain, is at the end of the continental rise.

18. A huge underwater mountain is called a _____.

19. A V-shaped valley below the ocean is known as a _____.

20. The mountain range rising above the ocean floor of the Atlantic Ocean is known as the _____.

How Do We Explore the Oceans?

21. Scientists explore the ocean with a _____ map by tracing the patterns of sonar echoes.

22. _____ are formed when seawater trickles down into the hot, newly formed oceanic crust saturated with minerals.

How Do People Affect the Oceans?

23. Offshore drilling for oil and _____ harms the environment.

What Causes Ocean Currents?

The map below shows the major ocean currents of the world. Read each label and note the color of the arrows.

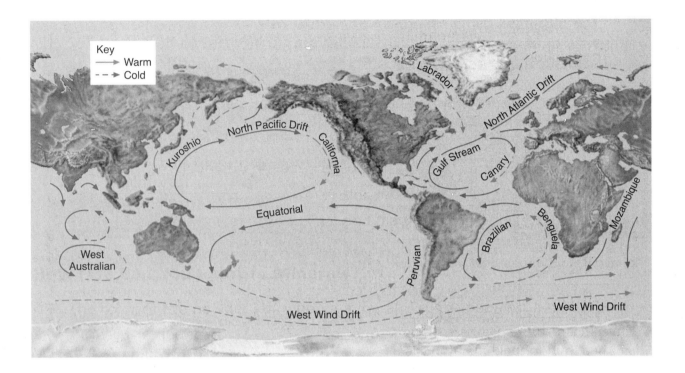

Answer the following questions about the map above.

1. What is the name of the most important warm current flowing along the Atlantic coast of North America?

    _____

    _____

2. What effect does the California Current have on the West Coast of the United States?

    _____

    _____

3. What is the name of the most important warm current that flows along the Atlantic coast of South America?

    _____

    _____

©Macmillan/McGraw-Hill

How Does the Water in a Wave Move?

The illustration below shows the movement of a wave, water particle motion, and the wave's direction.

Wave movement

Water particle motion

Answer the following questions about the picture above.

1. In what direction does the water particle move as the wave passes over it?

   _____

   _____

2. What happens to each water particle as a wave passes through the ocean?

   _____

   _____

3. What brings energy to the ocean water?

   _____

   _____

©Macmillan/McGraw-Hill

Earth's Oceans

Fill in the blanks.

1. The ocean's _____, or floor, contains mountains, valleys, and plains.

2. The _____ leads from the continental shelf toward the sea floor.

3. A stream of water that flows through the ocean like a river is called a(n) _____.

4. A buildup of sediment on the sea floor at the bottom of the continental slope is called the _____.

5. A huge underwater mountain is called a(n) _____.

6. The underwater edge of a continent is the _____.

7. A narrow v-shaped valley on the ocean floor is known as a _____.

8. The _____ are chains of mountains that wind their way through all the world's major oceans.

9. Vast, flat land covering almost half of the deep ocean floor is called the _____.

Answer each question.

10. What percentage of fish species are being overfished? _____

11. Where does marine pollution come from?

_____

_____

Earth's Oceans

Vocabulary

circles	currents	denser	Surface
Deep-water	meters	resurface	bend

Fill in the blanks.

Earth's rotation affects surface _____. This causes currents to

_____ to the right in the Northern Hemisphere and to the

left in the Southern Hemisphere. The currents start flowing in huge

_____. _____ currents move at a speed of

about 220 kilometers a day. _____ currents are set in motion

by differences in the temperature and saltiness of water. Colder, saltier water

is _____ than the water below it and slowly sinks toward the

ocean bottom. The water in a deep-water current moves much slower than

the water in a surface current, just a few _____ a day. The

water may not _____ for another 500 years.

Energy Resources

Fill in the blanks. Reading Skill: **Draw Conclusions** - questions 7, 14, 18

How Are Fossil Fuels Turned into Energy?

1. Energy to heat homes and run many common devices such as lights, computers, radios, TVs, and washers comes from _____.

2. Electricity from power plants comes to homes through _____.

3. Most vehicles get their energy from burning _____.

4. Heat from fossil fuels is used to boil water and turn it into _____ in order to generate electricity.

5. When the steam is released, it is directed to a big, pinwheel-like _____.

6. The spinning turbine turns a _____ to make electricity.

7. There are two disadvantages to fossil fuels: they are _____, meaning they cannot be replaced, and they _____ the environment.

Where Do Fossil Fuels Come From?

8. Fossil fuels are the remains of _____.

9. The source of energy in fossil fuels can be traced back to the _____.

10. The world's largest consumer of energy is _____.

Fill in the blanks.

What Other Sources of Energy Are There?

11. Sources of energy other than the burning of fossil fuels are called

    _____ energy sources.

12. Hydroelectric plants use running or falling _____ to spin a

    _____ to make electricity.

13. Earth's internal heat, or _____, can be used to heat

    homes and produce electricity.

14. Plants harness the Sun's energy through the process of _____.

15. A house can be heated when sunlight is trapped by _____

    _____, or collectors.

16. Devices that convert sunlight into electric energy are called

    _____.

How Can We Conserve Energy?

17. Conserving energy means not _____ what we have and

    using as _____ as possible.

18. We can also use _____ like water, wind,

    and solar energy.

19. Renewable energy from plant matter and animal wastes is

    called _____.

How Are Fossil Fuels Turned into Energy?

This diagram shows how most homes get their energy. It shows a picture of a power plant, power lines, a transformer, and a home.

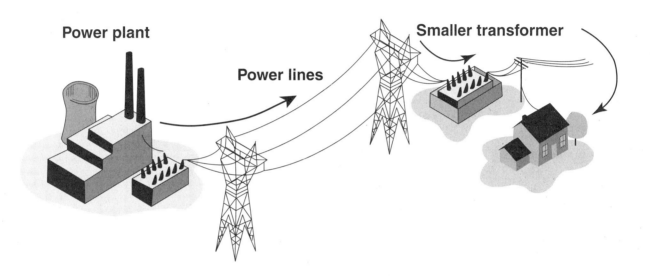

Power plant

Power lines

Smaller transformer

Answer these questions about the diagram above.

1. Where do homes get their energy?

   _____

2. How does energy get from the power plant to a house?

   _____

3. How do the wires change after the electricity goes through the smaller transformer?

   _____

   _____

© Macmillan/McGraw-Hill

Where Do Fossil Fuels Come From?

This diagram shows the process of microscopic plants and animals forming gas and oil over millions of years. Be sure you identify what happened and what caused it to happen.

HOW FOSSIL FUELS ARE FORMED

Ocean floor

Ancient ocean

Dead plants and animals fall to the ocean floor.

Ancient ocean

Dead plants and animals are covered with layers of sand and mud.

Ocean floor

Gas
Oil

Over millions of years, pressure and heat helped to turn the dead plant and animal remains into oil and natural gas.

Answer these questions about the diagram above.

1. Where do oil and natural gas come from?

_____

2. Where did this change take place?

_____

3. What happened in the ocean after the microscopic plants and animals fell to the floor?

_____

4. What forces act over millions of years to produce oil and natural gas?

_____

© Macmillan/McGraw - Hill

Energy Resources

Match the correct letter with the description.

_____ 1. energy from plant matter or animal wastes

_____ 2. called an inexhaustible source of energy

_____ 3. Earth's internal heat

_____ 4. uses moving water to produce electricity

_____ 5. energy from the Sun

_____ 6. coal, oil, and natural gas that come from plants and animals that died long ago

_____ 7. caused by burning fossil fuels

_____ 8. a source of energy other than the burning of a fossil fuel

Vocabulary

a. alternative energy source
b. geothermal energy
c. biomass
d. fossil fuels
e. air pollution
f. Sun
g. hydroelectric plant
h. solar energy

Answer each question.

9. List three ways you are using energy right now.

_____

_____

_____

10. List three ways you can conserve energy.

_____

_____

© Macmillan/McGraw-Hill

Energy Resources

Vocabulary

conserve	wind	alternative	generator	renewable
sunlight	steam	biomass	geothermal energy	

Fill in the blanks.

Fossil fuel supplies are limited since they aren't a(n) _____ energy source. We need to _____ energy supplies so they're not exhausted. One _____ energy source is the waterwheel. It can be used in a hydroelectric plant, where water spins a(n) _____. Moving air or _____ also can be harnessed for electricity. The _____ from water heated by _____ produces electricity. Solar cells convert _____ into electric energy. Another form of energy comes from _____, or plant and animal wastes.

Air, Water, and Energy

Circle the letter of the best answer.

1. A resource that can be replaced in a short period of time is
   - **a.** alternative.
   - **b.** fossil.
   - **c.** nonrenewable.
   - **d.** renewable.

2. A layer of gas in the atmosphere that screens out much of the Sun's UV rays is called the
   - **a.** air cycle.
   - **b.** aquifer.
   - **c.** ozone layer.
   - **d.** reservoir.

3. A fuel formed from the decay of ancient forms of life is a(n)
   - **a.** alternative fuel.
   - **b.** biomass.
   - **c.** fossil fuel.
   - **d.** geothermal fuel.

4. A mixture of smoke and fog is called
   - **a.** acid rain.
   - **b.** biomass.
   - **c.** ozone.
   - **d.** smog.

5. Moisture that falls to Earth after being mixed with wastes from burned fossil fuels is
   - **a.** acid rain.
   - **b.** groundwater.
   - **c.** biomass.
   - **d.** the water cycle.

6. Getting fresh water from seawater is
   - **a.** conservation.
   - **b.** deposition.
   - **c.** desalination.
   - **d.** purification.

7. The continuous movement of water between Earth's surface and the air is the
   - **a.** geothermal cycle.
   - **b.** ozone layer.
   - **c.** water cycle.
   - **d.** water table.

Circle the letter of the best answer.

8. Water that seeps into the ground into spaces between bits of rock and soil is
   a. groundwater.
   b. reservoir water.
   c. spring water.
   d. well water.

9. The top of the water-filled spaces in the ground is the
   a. ozone layer.
   b. reservoir.
   c. water cycle.
   d. water table.

10. An underground layer of rock or soil filled with water is the
    a. aquifer.
    b. groundwater.
    c. reservoir.
    d. water table.

11. A place where groundwater seeps out of the ground is a(n)
    a. aquifer.
    b. spring.
    c. water table.
    d. well.

12. A hole dug below the water table that water seeps into is a(n)
    a. aquifer.
    b. reservoir.
    c. spring.
    d. well.

13. A storage area for freshwater supplies is a(n)
    a. aquifer.
    b. reservoir.
    c. spring.
    d. well.

14. Earth's internal heat is called
    a. biomass.
    b. fossil fuel.
    c. geothermal energy.
    d. hydroelectric power.

Use Words

Word Box					
weathering	luster	lithosphere	smog	pollution	lava
hydrosphere	geologist	trench	inertia	humus	magma

Read each question below. Write your answer on the line. Use a word from the box.

1. Which word identifies melted rock deep below Earth's surface? _____

2. Which word means "the way light bounces off a mineral's surface"?

   _____

3. Which word identifies a scientist who studies Earth? _____

4. Which word identifies all of Earth's water? _____

5. Which word identifies magma that reaches Earth's surface? _____

6. Which word describes rocks breaking down into smaller pieces?

   _____

7. Which word means "a long, narrow V-shaped valley in the ocean"?

   _____

8. Which word describes a mixture of smoke and fog? _____

9. Which word identifies the tendency of a moving object to keep moving?

   _____

10. Which word means the decayed plant or animal material in soil?

    _____

11. Which word describes the hard outer layer of Earth? _____

12. Which word describes harmful substances added to Earth's land, water, or air?

    _____

Scrambled Words

Read each clue, then unscramble the letters and write the word correctly. Use the Word Box to check your spelling.

Word Box				
desalination	aquifer	fossil	planet	magma
crust	gravity	geologist	reservoir	meteorite

1. melted underground rock   gamma _____

2. a layer above Earth's mantle   struc _____

3. Mars or Earth   leapnt _____

4. a force that pulls things down   vargtiy _____

5. imprint or remains of living   silsof _____
   things of the past

6. someone who studies Earth   togglesoi _____

7. storage area for freshwater supplies rivoreser _____

8. rock from space that strikes Earth   trimoteee _____

9. underground rock filled with water   fraquie _____

10. getting freshwater from seawater   nationalside _____

Now mix up the letters of four more words from this unit. Write a clue for each word, then ask a friend to unscramble it.

1. _____

2. _____

3. _____

4. _____

©Macmillan/McGraw-Hill

Word Webs

Remember that a word web lists words that describe or relate to the same thing. Here is a web for the word *lava*.

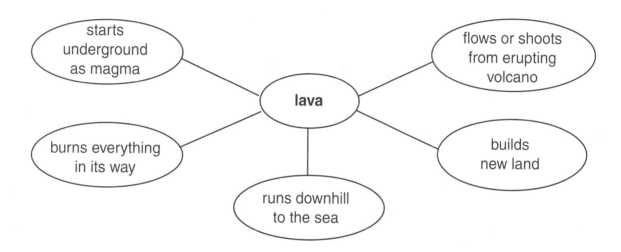

Now choose a vocabulary word or phrase, such as *biomass, solar energy, pollution, resource,* or *seamount.* Make a web with other words that relate to or describe it.

Weather

Find the main idea of this activity about weather. Fill in the circles and the blanks with the correct processes and supporting details. Then describe the main idea in the space provided.

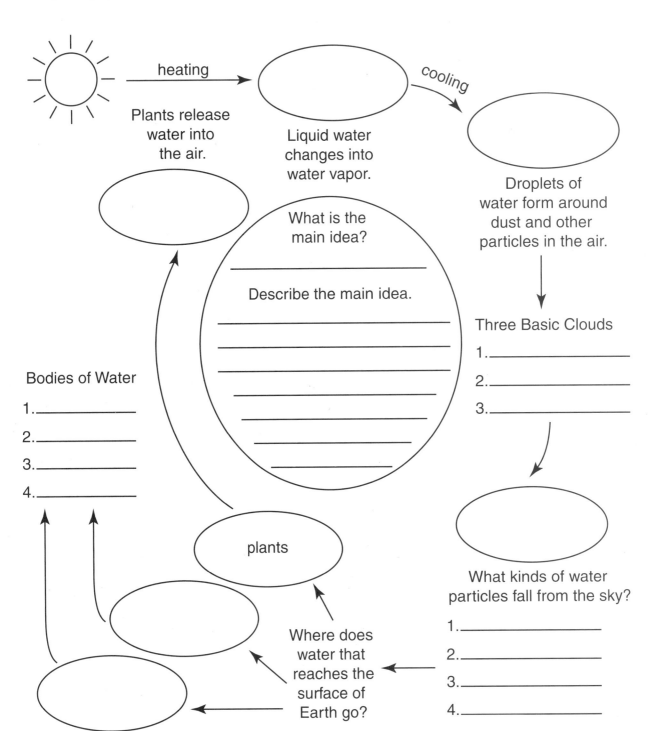

heating

Plants release water into the air.

Liquid water changes into water vapor.

cooling

Droplets of water form around dust and other particles in the air.

What is the main idea?

_____

Describe the main idea.

_____
_____
_____
_____
_____
_____

Three Basic Clouds

1._____
2._____
3._____

Bodies of Water

1._____
2._____
3._____
4._____

plants

Where does water that reaches the surface of Earth go?

What kinds of water particles fall from the sky?

1._____
2._____
3._____
4._____

©Macmillan/McGraw-Hill

Main Idea

Every story has a main idea, a sentence that tells what the story's mostly about. Other facts in the story are details that support, or tell more about, the main idea. Read the following paragraphs, based on information from this chapter of your textbook. Then circle the main idea and underline the supporting details in each paragraph.

1. What happens to the Sun as time goes by each day? In the morning the Sun is close to the horizon. By noon the Sun is high in the sky above you, as high as it gets all day. After noon the Sun begins to get lower and lower in the sky until it seems to disappear below the horizon.

2. Air temperature drops with altitude at about 2°C (3.5°F) every 305 meters (1,000 feet). For example, in Lewiston, Maine, elevation 34 meters (110 feet), it's a pleasant 21°C (70°F). Two hours away in Mount Washington, New Hampshire, elevation 1,917 meters (6,288 feet), it's only 1°C (34°F).

Now reread the Science Magazine article "Flood: Good News or Bad?" Then write the main idea of the article, and list at least four supporting details.

Main Idea: _____

_____

Supporting Details:

1. _____

_____

2. _____

_____

3. _____

_____

4. _____

_____

©Macmillan/McGraw-Hill

More Ideas and Details

Read the following paragraph about the monsoons. Then circle the main idea, and underline each of the supporting details.

> Why do the monsoons change direction? In summer the Sun heats dry air over tropical land, while nearby oceans stay cooler. The warm air rises above the land, and cooler air over the ocean blows in to take its place. The ocean wind brings heavy rain to the land. An area may get as much as 2.54 meters (100 inches) of rain a month! Then in winter the Sun heats the land less, so it cools off. As warm air rises over the ocean, dry cool wind from the land blows out to take its place. That same land area may get only 2.54 centimeters (1 inch) a month!

Now write a main idea and some supporting details about clouds, air pressure, the atmosphere, the water cycle, relative humidity, sea and land breezes, or some other weather condition. Give your paper to a classmate, and have him or her use the information to write a paragraph.

Main Idea: _____

_____

Supporting Details:

_____

_____

_____

_____

©Macmillan/McGraw-Hill

Atmosphere and Air Temperature

Fill in the blanks. 📖 Reading Skill: **Main Idea** - questions 2, 9, 16

Does the Sun's Angle Matter?

1. The hottest parts of Earth are the areas near _____, while the coldest are the areas _____.

2. The angle of the Sun's rays is the cause of differences in temperatures at the _____ and the _____.

3. Combining parts of the words "incoming," "solar," "radiation," forms the term "_____."

4. The greater the angle of insolation, the _____ a place will be.

What Affects Insolation?

5. The Sun is highest in the sky at _____.

6. The angle of insolation can be measured by examining the angles created by _____.

Why Do Some Things Get Hotter than Others?

7. In the same light, dark-colored materials get _____ than light-colored materials.

8. A rough surface gets _____ than a smooth surface because it absorbs more _____.

Why Do You Cool Down as You Go Up?

9. Air temperatures drop as you go higher up a mountain because you are traveling higher above _____.

10. Temperatures drop about _____ degrees for every _____ in altitude.

11. The troposphere is the lowest layer of Earth's _____.

©Macmillan/McGraw-Hill

What Happens to the Air Pressure?

12. As you go higher in altitude, _____ decreases steadily.

13. Air is made up mostly of _____ of the gases _____ and _____.

14. Normal air pressure is greatest at _____, because the _____ is tallest there.

15. Besides gases, air contains _____ and _____.

What Is Weather?

16. The term "weather" really describes what conditions are like in the _____ at a given place and time.

17. Besides temperature and air pressure, weather characteristics that change are

    a. _____,

    b. _____,

    c. _____, and

    d. _____.

18. Thermometers measure temperature by either the _____ or the _____ scale.

19. In a mercury barometer, _____ pushes mercury up in a tube.

20. A spring inside an accordion-like metal can measures air pressure in a(n) _____ barometer.

Does the Sun's Angle Matter?

Diagrams like this one take careful study. Notice the direction of the arrows, which show how Earth moves around the Sun during a year. Then notice that the diagram shows Earth's position and tilt relative to the Sun at different times of the year. To understand the diagram, look carefully at the changes from season to season. Observe the differences in the angle at which the Sun's rays fall on different parts of Earth.

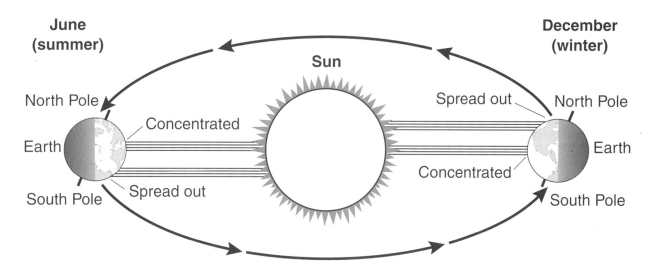

June (summer)

North Pole
Concentrated
Earth
South Pole
Spread out

Sun

December (winter)

Spread out
North Pole
Earth
Concentrated
South Pole

Answer these questions about the diagram above.

1. In December, which half of Earth, northern or southern, is tilted away from the Sun?

   _____

   Are the Sun's rays more or less concentrated in that half in December?

   _____

2. In June, is the southern half of Earth tilted toward or away from the Sun?

   _____

3. What part of Earth receives concentrated sunlight all year round?

   _____

4. Where on Earth are the Sun's rays spread out thinly all the time?

   _____

Why Do You Cool Down as You Go Up?

The two parts of this diagram show different, but related, kinds of information. To understand it, you need to look carefully at how the two parts are related. The left-hand part shows the layers of the atmosphere and their heights above the Earth. The other part is a graph of temperature change in each layer. Read it as you would read a line graph.

The Layers of the Atmosphere

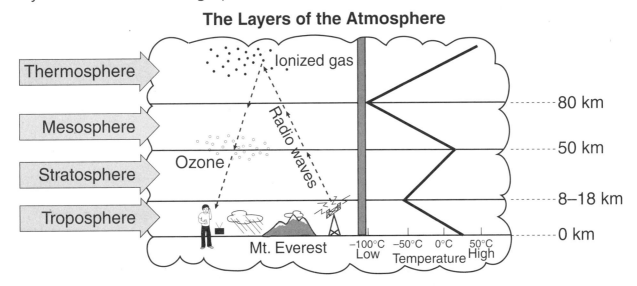

Answer these questions about the diagram above.

1. In what layer of the atmosphere do people live and clouds form?

   _____

   At about what height is the top of that layer? _____

2. Describe the location of the ozone layer.

   _____

3. Do temperatures get warmer or colder as you move from the lower stratosphere to the top of that layer? _____

   How big is the change? _____

4. The topmost layer of the atmosphere is the _____.

   How high above Earth does this layer begin? _____

5. Which layer has the greatest temperature change? _____

Atmosphere and Air Temperature

Fill in the blanks.

1. The air that surrounds the Earth is the _____.

2. Ninety-nine percent of the air we breathe is made up of _____ and _____.

3. Air pressure is measured by a(n) _____.

4. The levels of the four layers of the atmosphere are determined by sudden changes in _____ at each level.

5. The amount of the Sun's energy that reaches Earth at a given place and time is _____.

6. All the moisture around Earth is in the _____.

7. The force put on a given area by the weight of the air above it is _____.

8. The conditions present in the troposphere at any given time determine the _____.

Vocabulary

insolation
weather
nitrogen
air pressure
troposphere
barometer
oxygen
atmosphere
temperature

Answer each question.

9. How does air pressure change with altitude? Why?

_____

_____

10. What happens to temperature as the angle at which the Sun's rays strike Earth's surface increases? As the angle decreases? What happens to the length of shadows at the same time?

_____

_____

_____

11. What color would you choose to wear if it were 95° and you wanted to stay as cool as possible? Why?

_____

Atmosphere and Air Temperature

Vocabulary

thermometer	Celsius	air pressure
weight	aneroid	air
spring	changes	barometer

Fill in the blanks.

You can measure temperature using a _____. The

temperature is read on a Fahrenheit or a(n) _____

scale. _____ can be measured using a mercury

_____, which has a glass tube with the open end

submerged in liquid mercury. The mercury stops rising when its

_____ equals the air pressure. You also can use a(n)

_____ barometer to measure air pressure. This device is

an accordion-like metal can with most of the _____

removed. Inside, a(n) _____ balances the outside air

pressure. A needle indicates the _____ in air pressure.

Water Vapor and Humidity

Fill in the blanks. Reading Skill: **Main Idea** - questions 2, 11, 19

Where Does Water Vapor Come From?

1. When water drops form on a cold glass, the water comes from the _____.

2. Water vapor is water in the form of a(n) _____.

3. The amount of water in the air is _____.

4. Water covers more than _____ of Earth's surface.

5. Liquid water becomes a gas called water vapor through the process of _____.

6. The Sun's energy enables _____ from the water's surface to escape into the atmosphere.

7. The change from a gas to a liquid is called _____.

8. The second-largest source of water vapor is _____ from plant leaves.

What Is Relative Humidity?

9. Humidity is measured in grams per _____.

10. If water is available, warm air will take on _____ water vapor than cold air.

11. Relative humidity is a comparison between how much _____ is in the air and how much the air could hold.

12. Fifty-percent relative humidity means that air is holding _____ of what it could if it were full.

13. The relative humidity of your air depends upon changes in your _____.

14. When relative humidity is high, less _____ can evaporate from your skin.

15. When warm air is _____, the water vapor in it condenses.

16. Clouds and rain are more likely when the relative humidity is _____.

What Happens When Warm, Moist Air Cools?

17. Whenever warm air rises higher in the sky, it _____.

18. When cool and warm air meet, the lighter _____ is pushed up over the heavier, cold air.

19. Whenever warm air rises and cools, the water vapor in the air _____.

20. Water droplets in the air form _____.

What Is Relative Humidity?

This graph shows how, at 100% humidity, the amount of water vapor in a given volume of air changes with temperature. It demonstrates that humidity—the amount of water vapor in the air—changes as the temperature goes up and down. To understand a graph like this one, begin by carefully reading all the labels. Be sure you know exactly what is being measured and what each symbol represents. Notice that little glasses of water are used to form the bars of the graph.

Answer these questions about the diagram above.

1. The horizontal axis of this graph measures _____.

2. This graph measures the number of _____ of water vapor in a(n) _____ of air.

3. On this graph, one large glass of water stands for _____ grams of water per cubic meter or air.

4. At a temperature of 25°C, about how much water vapor can a cubic meter of air hold?

   _____

5. Can air at a temperature of 35°C hold more or less water vapor than air at a temperature of 15°C?

   _____

How Clouds Form

These three diagrams show three ways in which clouds are formed when water vapor in the air condenses. When air moves higher, it cools. Because the temperature decreases, condensation from water droplets is greater than evaporation from the droplet. As a result, the droplets grow. The diagrams show what can happen next.

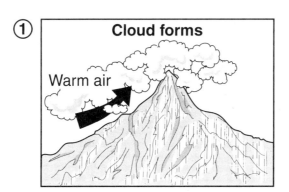

① **Cloud forms**

Warm air

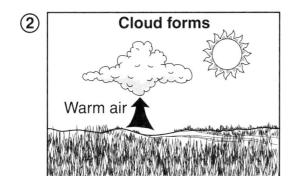

② **Cloud forms**

Warm air

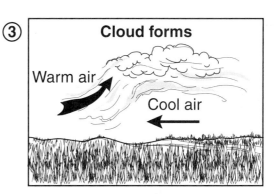

③ **Cloud forms**

Warm air

Cool air

Answer these questions about the diagram above.

1. In diagram 1, does the air get warmer or cooler when the wind pushes it up over the mountain? _____

2. What happens to the water vapor in the air when the air cools?

    _____

3. In diagram 2, the Sun warms the ground. What happens to the warm air near the ground?

    _____

4. In diagram 3, the warm air is pushed up by the _____ below it.

© Macmillan/McGraw-Hill

Water Vapor and Humidity

Fill in the blanks.

humidity

evaporation

relative humidity

condensation

transpiration

water vapor

1. The amount of water vapor in the air is called the
_____.

2. The changing of a liquid into a gas is called _____.

3. Water in the form of a gas is _____.

4. The changing of a gas into a liquid is
_____.

5. A comparison between how much water vapor is in
the air and how much the air could hold is
called _____.

6. The leaves of plants release water vapor into the air
through _____.

Answer each question.

7. What is relative humidity?

_____

_____

8. What two factors determine the amount of humidity in the air?

_____

_____

_____

9. What effect does temperature have on evaporation?

_____

_____

10. When does condensation occur?

_____

_____

Water Vapor and Humidity

Vocabulary

humidity	evaporate	water vapor	gas	two-thirds
oceans	trillions	plants	absorb	evaporation

Fill in the blanks.

The water in the air is _____. Water vapor is water in the

form of _____. _____ is the amount of

water vapor in the air. More than _____ of planet Earth is

covered with liquid water from _____, rivers, and lakes.

There is also water in the ground, and in _____. The

changing of liquid water into a gas is called _____. Each

day the Sun turns _____ of tons of ocean water into water

vapor. Water molecules _____ the Sun's energy and speed

up. "Speedy" water molecules near the surface of the liquid "escape" or

_____ in the atmosphere as water vapor.

Clouds and Precipitation

Fill in the blanks. Reading Skill: **Main Idea** - questions 2, 5

How Do Clouds Form?

1. Clouds are made up of _____ or _____.

2. All clouds form when the air cools and water vapor _____ around dust and other particles.

3. A thick, sharp-edged gray cloud is probably made of _____, not _____.

4. All clouds form in the lower atmosphere, or _____.

5. The three basic cloud forms are:
   a. blanketlike layers, or _____,
   b. puffy, flat-based _____, and
   c. high-altitude, feathery _____.

6. The prefix "nimbo-," or nimbus, as in nimbostratus, refers to a cloud that brings _____ or _____.

7. A cloud at ground level is called _____.

What Is Precipitation?

8. Any form of water particles that falls to the ground from the atmosphere is _____.

9. Precipitation occurs when water droplets or ice crystals join together and become _____.

10. A dust particle is the _____ around which water molecules condense.

11. The type of precipitation formed from ice crystals that occurs when the ground temperature is cold is _____.

12. When cloud droplets collect and freeze around an ice crystal, and the process repeats over and over, _____ is formed.

© Macmillan/McGraw-Hill

Fill in the blanks.

Are Cloud Type and Precipitation Related?

13. The shape and height of certain clouds determine the kind of
_____ that falls.

14. Rain or snow from large _____ clouds is likely to be heavier
but usually doesn't last as long as that from _____ clouds.

15. Heavy rain and sometimes _____ come from clouds whose tops
reach where it is below freezing.

16. Strong winds, or _____, inside a huge cloud move ice crystals
upward again and again.

What Is the Water Cycle?

17. Precipitation may reach rivers as _____ or seep into the ground
as _____.

18. In the water cycle, the processes of _____ and
_____ take water out of the atmosphere.

19. Water in the water cycle changes from liquid to _____ and
back to _____.

How Do You Record How Cloudy It Is?

20. A term like "overcast" refers to _____, the portion of the sky
covered by clouds.

21. In a weather station model, different amounts of cloud cover is shown by
_____.

©Macmillan/McGraw-Hill

What Is Precipitation?

Charts like this one organize information. This chart shows four different types of precipitation and how each one forms. To understand the chart, read the labels on each column. Then follow the arrows to see the steps in forming each kind of precipitation.

Types of Precipitation

Condensation around nucleus	Condensation around nucleus	Condensation around ice nucleus	Condensation around nucleus
Cloud droplets collect.	Cloud droplets collect.	Supercooled water freezes around ice nucleus or water vapor changes to ice crystals.	Cloud droplet
	Raindrop		Freezing
		Ice crystals grow larger.	Cloud droplets collect around ice crystal
		Snowflakes	Freezing
Fall through warm air	Fall through air at freezing temperature		Repeats over and over.
		Cold ground temperature	Warm ground temperature
Rain	**Sleet**	**Snow**	**Hail**

Answer these questions about the diagram above.

1. What first step do all types of precipitation have in common?

_____

2. When raindrops fall through air at freezing temperatures, they become

_____

3. What two things can happen after condensation forms around an ice nucleus?

_____

_____

4. A snowflake forms when _____ grow larger.

What Is the Water Cycle?

This diagram represents the water cycle. It shows the endless process as water moves to Earth's surface and back again into the atmosphere. Follow the arrows to track the different stages that water passes through during this cycle. Read the labels at every stage.

The Water Cycle

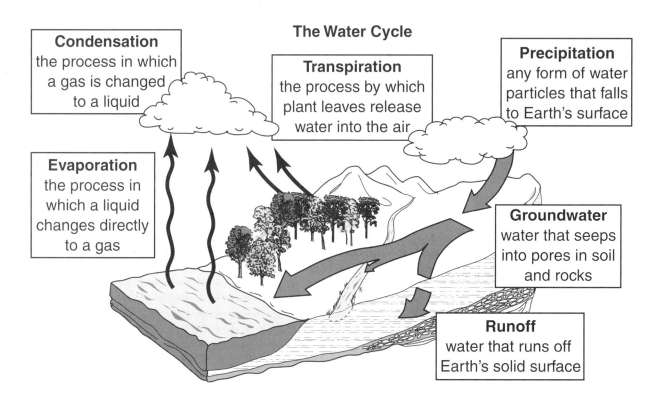

Condensation
the process in which a gas is changed to a liquid

Transpiration
the process by which plant leaves release water into the air

Precipitation
any form of water particles that falls to Earth's surface

Evaporation
the process in which a liquid changes directly to a gas

Groundwater
water that seeps into pores in soil and rocks

Runoff
water that runs off Earth's solid surface

Answer these questions about the diagram above.

1. When water falls as precipitation, it either runs off Earth's surface or sinks into the ground as _____.

2. The leaves of plants send water into the air in the process of _____.

3. Liquid water changes into a gas in the process of _____.

4. In the atmosphere, water vapor, a gas, becomes a(n) _____ by condensation.

©Macmillan/McGraw-Hill

Clouds and Precipitation

Fill in the blanks.

1. Moist air cooled at ground level causes _____ to form.

2. High-altitude clouds that look feather-like are _____ clouds.

3. Whether precipitation is rain or snow depends on the _____ in the atmosphere and on the ground.

4. A cloud that looks puffy but has a flat bottom is a(n) _____ cloud.

5. Rain, snow, sleet, and hail are all kinds of _____.

6. Clouds that form in blanketlike layers are _____ clouds.

7. The continuous movement of water between Earth's surface and the air is the _____.

Vocabulary

stratus

fog

cumulus

cirrus

temperature

water cycle

precipitation

Answer each question.

8. Describe the water cycle.

_____

_____

_____

_____

9. What happens to the precipitation that reaches Earth's surface?

_____

_____

10. What are the five terms used to describe how cloudy it is on a given day?

_____

_____

© Macmillan/McGraw-Hill

Clouds and Precipitation

cirrus	stratus	fog
height	nimbo	cumulonimbus
cumulus	troposphere	shape

Fill in the blanks.

Clouds are found only in the _____. Those that form in

blanketlike layers are _____ clouds. _____

clouds form at very high altitudes out of ice crystals. They have a featherlike

_____. Puffy clouds that seem to rise up from a flat bottom

are called _____ clouds. If snow or rain falls from a cloud, the

term _____ is added to the cloud's name. Clouds are further

grouped into families by form and _____. For example,

_____ clouds develop upward. A cloud at ground level is

called _____.

Air Pressure and Wind

Fill in the blanks. 📖 Reading Skill: **Main Idea** - questions 3, 13, 14

How Can Air Pressure Change?

1. If the volume of a container increases, the air pressure inside the container will _____.

2. Air pressure is _____ at sea level, than high in the atmosphere.

3. When air is heated, air pressure decreases because the molecules _____ and _____.

4. Air molecules in cold air exert _____ pressure than air molecules in warm air because they are closer together and collide more often.

5. Air contains the gases _____ and _____, which are heavier than molecules of water vapor. So, moist air exerts _____ pressure than dry air.

6. In a weather station model, a line slanting up and to the right shows that air pressure is _____.

Why Do Winds Blow?

7. When denser air moves toward less dense air, it creates _____.

8. Warm air rises because it is _____, or less dense.

9. Rising air is a(n) _____, while sinking air is a(n) _____.

10. Rising warm air and sinking cool air form a circular wind pattern called a(n) _____.

11. Convection cells form because of unequal _____ and _____ of the air.

Fill in the blanks.

What Are Sea and Land Breezes?

12. Land warms up _____ than water.

13. On a warm day, the air above the land _____, and a cool _____ blows toward the land.

14. At night, the land cools more quickly than the water, causing a(n) _____ to blow toward the water.

15. A valley breeze blows up a mountain slope because the air on the slope is _____.

What Is the Coriolis Effect?

16. Winds in the Northern Hemisphere seem to curve to the _____ because Earth is _____ under them.

How Are Global Wind Patterns Produced?

17. Warm, moist air over the equator creates a zone of _____, while cold dry air at the poles has _____.

18. Global wind zones are set up by air moving from zones of _____ to zones of _____.

19. Global winds seem to travel in curved paths because of the _____.

What Are Isobars?

20. A line on a weather map connecting locations with equal air pressure is called a(n) _____.

How Do We Study the Wind?

21. The spinning cups of a(n) _____ help measure wind speed.

How Can Air Pressure Change?

This diagram illustrates an experiment showing that volume is one factor that causes changes in air pressure. It shows two jars with a plastic bag fastened over their tops. Look at the jars and notice the difference between the air molecules inside them. Then study the smaller diagrams, which show the pressures inside and outside the jars.

An Air Pressure Model

Answer these questions about the diagram above.

1. In the jar on the left, is the inside air pressure greater than, less than, or the same as the outside air pressure? _____

2. Pulling up the plastic bag on the right-hand jar increases the _____ inside the bag-jar system.

3. Are the air molecules in the right-hand jar closer together or farther apart than those in the other jar? _____

4. When the volume increases, the air pressure in the jar becomes _____ than the air pressure outside.

What Are Sea and Land Breezes?

Land temperatures change faster than water temperatures do. This diagram shows how those temperature changes can affect winds and wind directions along a coastline. This diagram shows how a sea breeze—a breeze that blows from the ocean—is created during the day.

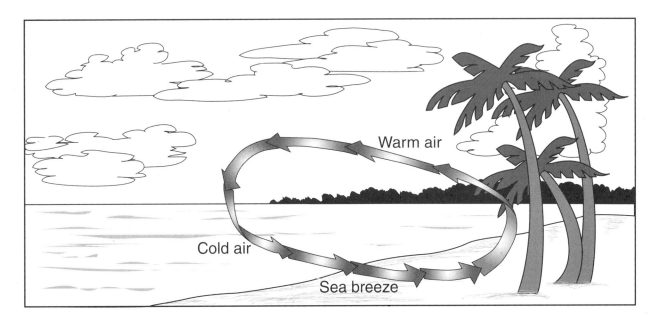

Answer these questions about the diagram above.

1. On a sunny day, does the air over land get warmer or cooler than the air over the water? _____

2. In what direction does the warmer air move? _____

3. When a sea breeze blows, it brings _____ air to the land.

4. This diagram shows why a sea breeze blows inland during the day. Now figure out what will happen to these wind patterns at night. Remember that land temperatures change faster than water temperatures. Explain what you think will happen.

_____

_____

Air Pressure and Wind

Fill in the blanks.

1. Air that moves horizontally is called _____.

2. A breeze that blows from sea to land is a(n) _____.

3. A device that measures air speed is a(n) _____.

4. A line on a map connecting places with equal air pressure is a(n) _____.

5. A breeze that blows from land to sea is a(n) _____.

6. A device used to tell wind direction is called a(n) _____.

7. In the Northern hemisphere the wind curves to the right; this curving is called the _____.

8. The pattern of air rising, sinking, and blowing horizontally is a(n) _____.

Vocabulary

weather vane
convection cell
Coriolis effect
wind
isobar
land breeze
sea breeze
anemometer

Answer each question.

9. What are some of the factors that might interrupt the wind blowing in a straight line forever?

_____

_____

10. Compare the air pressure at sea level with the air pressure on top of a mountain. Why are the two pressures different?

_____

_____

_____

© Macmillan/McGraw-Hill

Air Pressure and Wind

Vocabulary

compass	speedometer	tip	shaft
anemometer	weather vane	pointer	pinwheel

Fill in the blanks.

You can tell wind direction by looking at a _____. This device

has a(n) _____ that blows around in the wind. It's mounted

so it can indicate the four different _____ markings. When

the wind blows, it exerts more pressure on the tail than the

_____. A device called a(n) _____ measures

wind speed. This is a series of cups mounted on a(n) _____

that spins. When the cups whirl, they resemble a(n) _____.

A(n) _____ is calibrated to measure wind speed.

Weather

Circle the letter of the best answer.

1. As you get higher in altitude, air pressure
   - **a.** increases.
   - **b.** remains the same.
   - **c.** decreases.
   - **d.** rises.

2. Which layer of the atmosphere is farthest from Earth?
   - **a.** thermosphere
   - **b.** stratosphere
   - **c.** mesosphere
   - **d.** troposphere

3. Which is NOT a part of the water cycle?
   - **a.** evaporation
   - **b.** condensation
   - **c.** photosynthesis
   - **d.** precipitation

4. When weather is described as overcast
   - **a.** there are no clouds.
   - **b.** the entire sky is covered by clouds.
   - **c.** there are a few clouds in the sky.
   - **d.** the sky is half covered by clouds.

5. Insolation is
   - **a.** the amount of the Sun's rays that reach Earth.
   - **b.** the angle at which the Sun's rays hit Earth.
   - **c.** the insulating effect of the atmosphere.
   - **d.** another name for the mesosphere.

6. An instrument used to measure air speed is a(n)
   - **a.** thermometer.
   - **b.** barometer.
   - **c.** gauge.
   - **d.** anemometer.

7. Weather is determined by the conditions in the
   - **a.** thermosphere.
   - **b.** mesoshpere.
   - **c.** troposphere.
   - **d.** stratosphere.

8. Humidity is

   a. found mostly along shorelines.

   b. how much moisture the air could hold if it was warm.

   c. the amount of moisture in the air.

   d. the amount of moisture at ground level.

9. A falling barometer indicates

   a. a storm is coming.

   b. nice weather is coming.

   c. air pressure is rising.

   d. a sea breeze is present.

10. A circular pattern of updrafts, downdrafts, and winds is a(n)

   a. weather pattern.   b. convection cell.

   c. Coriolis effect.   d. isobar.

11. Wind is air that moves

   a. vertically.   b. in a circular pattern.

   c. horizontally.   d. down.

12. Cumulonimbus clouds are

   a. pretty, fluffy clouds.

   b. clouds that bring thunderstorms.

   c. whispy clouds made of ice crystals.

   d. clouds at ground level.

13. Which is NOT a form of precipitation?

   a. rain   b. snow

   c. hail   d. water droplets

14. Rain is measured in

   a. inches.   b. kilometers.

   c. buckets.   d. cats and dogs.

Chapter Summary

1. What is the name of the chapter you just finished reading?

   _____

   _____

2. What are four vocabulary words you learned in the chapter?
   Write a definition for each.

   _____

   _____

   _____

   _____

   _____

   _____

   _____

   _____

3. What are two main ideas that you learned in this chapter?

   _____

   _____

   _____

   _____

   _____

   _____

©Macmillan/McGraw-Hill

Weather Patterns and Climate

Listed below are 12 events that occur during a thunderstorm. Put the events in the proper order from beginning to end. Starting with the beginning of a thunderstorm, write the number of each event in the correct circle.

1. Heavy rain turns to light rain and then stops.

2. An upward rush of air called an updraft causes clouds to form.

3. Falling rain causes air to move downward in a downdraft.

4. A large buildup of static electricity releases a huge spark called lightning.

5. Air expands with such force that it creates a very loud sound called thunder.

6. Heavy rain or hail falls to the ground.

7. Intense heating causes warm, moist air to rise quickly.

8. Updrafts can no longer support water droplets or ice crystals.

9. Downdrafts become stronger than updrafts.

10. Falling air rubbing against rising air causes static electricity to build up.

11. Updrafts continue, causing clouds and water droplets to grow larger and larger.

12. Lightning superheats the air, causing it to expand suddenly.

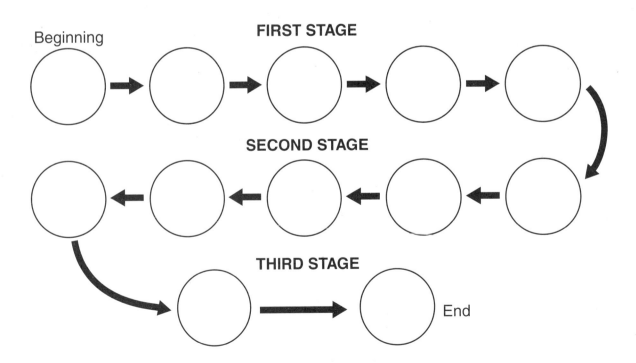

FIRST STAGE

Beginning

SECOND STAGE

THIRD STAGE

End

©Macmillan/McGraw-Hill

Sequence of Events

Everything in life happens in sequence. You can't have your 13th birthday until you've had your 12th birthday, you can't eat pizza until it comes out of the oven, and you can't wake up until you go to sleep!

Read each example below. Then answer the questions.

1. The money we raised at the bake sale paid for our trip to Washington.

   What happened first?   _____

   What happened second?   _____

2. We had a victory celebration after our team won the championship game.

   What happened first?   _____

   What happened second?   _____

3. I had to baby-sit my cousin in the morning, but later I baked cookies and took them to Pat's party.

   What happened first?   _____

   What happened next?   _____

   What happened last?   _____

4. I read the book, then researched the author on the Internet, and finally finished my report at 10 P.M.!

   What happened first?   _____

   What happened next?   _____

   What happened last?   _____

5. We set up our tents and went swimming. After lunch we went hiking in the woods.

   What happened first?   _____

   What happened next?   _____

   What happened next?   _____

   What happened last?   _____

© Macmillan/McGraw-Hill

In Sequence

Everything happens in sequence. Number these steps, based on the time line in the Science Magazine article "Weather Watch: Then and Now," to show the order in which things happened.

_____ The new telegraph system is used to collect weather data.

_____ Aristotle tries to explain rain, snow, and other "meteors" from the sky!

_____ The barometer is invented.

_____ NASA sends up the first weather satellite.

_____ Four Norwegian scientists use math and physics to identify
weather patterns.

_____ Two kinds of satellites track weather patterns. One monitors changes in
storm systems, and the other gives details about clouds.

_____ Doppler radar is developed.

_____ Benjamin Franklin predicts the weather.

_____ Radar tracks storms during World War II.

Now write the sequence of events for (1) an occluded front, (2) a stationary front, (3) a thunderstorm, (4) a tornado, or (5) a hurricane.

_____

_____

_____

_____

_____

©Macmillan/McGraw-Hill

Air Masses and Fronts

Fill in the blanks. Reading Skill: **Sequence of Events** - question 6, 16

How Do Air Masses Affect Weather?

1. A large region of the atmosphere where the air has similar properties throughout is called a(n) _____.

2. An air mass that forms over the warm water of the Gulf of Mexico will be _____ and _____.

3. Once an air mass forms, it is moved by _____.

4. In the United States, air masses generally move from _____ to _____.

5. At the boundary between air masses with different temperatures a(n) _____ forms.

How Do Fronts Affect Weather?

6. Cold air moves in under a warm air mass, often bringing winds and brief storms, in a(n) _____.

7. After a cold front passes, the weather is usually _____, _____, and _____.

8. Warm air moves up and over a cold air mass in a(n) _____.

9. Rainy days and warmer, more humid weather is brought by _____.

10. When a fast-moving cold front meets a warm front, a(n) _____ front forms.

11. In a cold-front occlusion, warm air is _____ between the incoming cold front and a region of cool air.

12. In a warm-front occlusion, the incoming air is _____, not cold.

13. When air masses meet and remain over a region, they produce a(n) _____.

Why Are Weather Satellites Important?

14. Photos taken by _____ can show weather patterns on Earth's surface.

15. Fronts are an important clue to _____.

16. Collisions between fronts can also be a warning about sudden _____.

Why Use Weather Records?

17. Scientists usually forecast the weather with a weather map that summarizes information from _____.

18. Statistical forecasting is based on _____.

How Do Air Masses Affect Weather?

This diagram shows how a weather front forms when warm and cold air masses meet. To understand a diagram like this, read all the labels. Notice the positions of the warm and cold air. Then follow the arrows to trace the movements of the different air masses.

A Weather Front

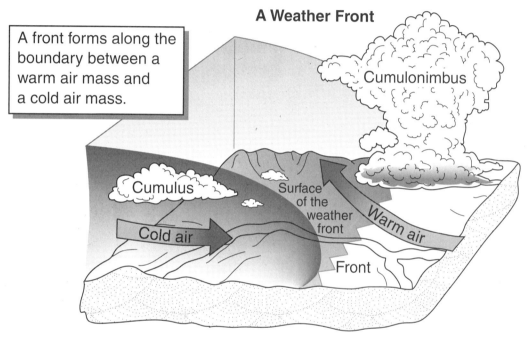

A front forms along the boundary between a warm air mass and a cold air mass.

Cumulonimbus

Cumulus

Surface of the weather front

Warm air

Cold air

Front

Answer these questions about the diagram above.

1. Is the cold air mass moving toward the left or the right side of the diagram?

   _____

2. How does the warm air move when it meets the cold air mass?

   _____

3. What kinds of clouds form where the warm air is rising?

   _____

4. What kind of clouds form behind the front?

   _____

5. What do the arrows along the front show?

   _____

How Do Fronts Affect Weather?

These diagrams show how two different kinds of fronts—a cold front and an occluded front—affect the weather in an area. Read all the labels. Notice the arrows that show the direction in which air masses are moving. Look for differences between the two kinds of fronts.

Weather Produced by Fronts

Cold front

Cold air Warm air

Colder, denser air moves in under a region of warm air.

Different fronts produce different kinds of weather. The weather along a front depends upon how the air masses interact.

Cold-front occlusion

Warm air Cold air Cool air

A cold front catches up with a warm front, pushing the warm air up and away.

Answer these questions about the diagram above.

1. In the diagram of a cold front, what happens to the warm air as the cold air mass moves in? _____

2. In the cold-front occlusion, is the cold air moving toward the left or right of the diagram? _____

3. In the second diagram, what kind of air is directly ahead of the moving cold air? _____

4. What has happened to the warm air mass in a cold-front occlusion?

_____

Air Masses and Fronts

Fill in the blanks.

cold

stationary

east

west

air mass

front

occluded

warm

1. A large region of the atmosphere where the air has similar properties throughout is called _____.

2. A narrow boundary between two air masses is called a(n) _____.

3. Brief, heavy storms are brought by _____ fronts.

4. When a cold front and warm front meet, _____ fronts form.

5. Light, steady rain or snow is brought by _____ fronts.

6. The global winds in the United States blow from _____ to _____.

7. When a cold air mass and a warm air mass meet and remain over an area for days without moving, it is called a(n) _____ front.

Answer each question.

8. Why are fronts so important to our everyday life?

_____

_____

_____

9. What do scientists use to help them predict weather?

_____

_____

_____

Air Masses and Fronts

Vocabulary

air mass	cold	snow	warm
occluded	drier	cooler	thunderstorm

Fill in the blanks.

In a(n) _____ front, cold air moves in under a warm

_____. Cold fronts often bring brief, heavy

_____ and strong winds. After the storm the skies are usually

clearer, and the weather is _____ and_____.

In a(n) _____ front, warm air moves in over a cold air mass.

Warm fronts often bring light, steady rain or _____. A(n)

_____ front occurs when a cold front and a warm front meet.

Severe Storms

Fill in the blanks. Reading Skill: **Sequence of Events** - questions 2, 3, 5

What Are Thunderstorms?

1. In the first stage of a thunderstorm, _____ move warm air upward in a cloud.

2. When there is too much water in a thunderstorm cloud, it falls as _____.

3. Falling rain causes _____ in a thunderstorm cloud, building up _____.

4. A spark between electric charges in a cloud is _____.

5. In the third stage of a thunderstorm, a _____ becomes stronger than the updraft.

6. Thunderstorms are likely to form in the warm air ahead of a(n) _____.

How and Where Do Tornadoes Happen?

7. Air rushes in from all sides when the updraft in a(n) _____ _____ is very strong.

8. As the air curves into a spin, the tornado gets stronger, and a(n) _____ forms.

9. Tornadoes form where dry, cold air masses mix with _____ _____.

10. The regions of the United States where tornadoes are most likely to occur are:
    a. _____ and
    b. _____.

11. A tornado over water forms a(n) _____.

How Do Hurricanes Form?

12. A hurricane is a large swirling storm with an area of very _____ at the center.

13. A low-pressure center forms in a hurricane because of strong heating and lots of _____ from the surface of warm ocean water.

14. When the wind nears the center, it moves upward and forms a(n) _____ of tall thunderstorms.

15. Winds spiral counterclockwise toward a low-pressure center, pulling in the thunderstorms, because of the _____.

16. Hurricanes have a wind speed of _____ or higher.

17. An area of light winds and clear skies at the center is the _____ of a hurricane.

How Do Hurricanes Affect Ocean Waves?

18. The low air pressure beneath a hurricane causes a rise in the sea called a(n) _____.

19. Hurricane Fran formed near _____ and struck the coast of _____ and _____.

20. Hurricanes die over land because they cannot gather more _____ from the ocean.

What Can You Do to Be Safe in a Storm?

21. A storm watch means that _____ are right for a storm, while a(n) _____ means that a storm is on its way.

How Can Radar Track Storms?

22. Doppler radar uses _____ to locate storms.

What Are Thunderstorms?

These three diagrams show the stages of a thunderstorm as it develops and then dies away. As with any diagram, it's important to start by reading all the labels and captions. Also remember that arrows usually show movement or steps in a process. Notice how the arrows change in each diagram.

Warm air rises

+ = Positive electric charge

− = Negative electric charge

Lightning   **Heavy rain**

+ + +

Light rain

① Strong updrafts form inside the cloud.

② Electric charges build up inside the cloud.

③ A thunderstorm dies when a downdraft becomes stronger than the updraft. Heavy rain lightens up and stops.

Answer these questions about the diagram above.

1. As a thunderstorm starts to form, updrafts carry _____ upward in a cloud.

2. When there is too much water for the updrafts to support, _____ falls from the cloud.

3. In the second stage of a thunderstorm, _____ and _____ electric charges build up in the cloud.

4. The spark that jumps between electric charges is _____.

5. Falling rain causes a(n) _____ in the cloud, which eventually ends the storm.

How Do Hurricanes Form?

This is a cutaway diagram. Such diagrams are used to show both the inside and the outside of something. Here, arrows show you the paths of different types of winds and air masses in a hurricane. Other arrows show how the hurricane moves. Study these movements and read the labels.

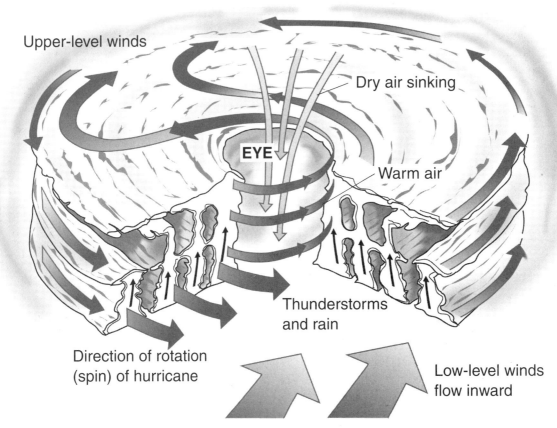

Upper-level winds

Dry air sinking

EYE

Warm air

Thunderstorms and rain

Direction of rotation (spin) of hurricane

Low-level winds flow inward

Answer these questions about the diagram above.

1. What forms at the center of the hurricane?

   _____

2. At the eye of the hurricane, _____ is sinking.

3. A hurricane spins in a(n) _____ direction.

4. Why do you think people are sometimes fooled by the eye of a hurricane?

   _____

   _____

   _____

Severe Storms

Fill in the blanks.

Vocabulary

thunderstorm

air pressure

cold front

tornado

storm surge

hurricane

1. A violent whirling wind that moves across the ground in a narrow path is called a(n) _____.

2. Low air pressure in a storm can cause a(n) _____, a bulge of water along the ocean shore.

3. A storm that forms over tropical oceans, near the equator is a(n) _____.

4. The center of a hurricane is characterized by very low _____.

5. The most common kind of severe storm is a _____.

6. Thunderstorms occur most frequently when the weather is hot and a(n) _____ approaches.

Answer each question.

7. How do strong updrafts contribute to the severity of a thunderstorm?

_____

_____

8. What is the difference between a hurricane and a tornado?

_____

_____

_____

_____

9. How can you protect yourself in a thunderstorm?

_____

_____

_____

© Macmillan/McGraw-Hill

Severe Storms

Vocabulary

noise	rise	cold	rains
lightning	thunderstorms	updrafts	down

Fill in the blanks.

_____ form in cumulonimbus clouds called thunderheads.

Huge electric sparks called _____ heat the air. This produces the

_____ named thunder. Thunderstorms usually feature strong

winds and heavy _____. Thunderstorms begin when strong

_____, or upward rushes of heated air, form inside clouds. Then

the rising air rubs against the air going _____, building up static

electricity. When the weather is hot and humid with a(n) _____

front approaching, thunderstorms are probable. These conditions cause the

warm air to _____ rapidly.

© Macmillan/McGraw-Hill

Climate

Fill in the blanks. Reading Skill: **Sequence of Events** - questions 9, 14

What Is Climate?

1. The average weather pattern of a region over time is its _____.

2. Two ways to describe a region's climate are:

   a. _____ and

   b. _____.

What Affects Climate?

3. Climate depends on factors that affect _____ and _____ over a period of time.

4. A measure of a place's distance north or south of the _____ is the degrees of _____.

5. The _____ at different latitudes causes differences in temperature.

6. The three climate zones that depend on latitude are

   a. _____, near the equator;

   b. _____, in the middle latitudes;

   c. _____, at high latitudes near the North and South Poles.

7. Land areas heat up and cool off _____ than water.

8. In winter, air temperatures over land are _____ than temperatures over water.

9. Winds set up _____ in the ocean, which move warm or cool water across the ocean surface.

10. Mountain ranges can block both cold air and _____.

How Does Earth Gain and Lose Energy?

11. Earth's surface both _____ heat from sunlight and _____ heat back into space.

12. If the energy gained from the Sun equals energy lost into space, the _____ on Earth stays the same.

13. Earth's atmosphere reflects about _____ of incoming sunlight and absorbs _____ more.

14. If there are few clouds, less heat is absorbed, and the night is _____.

15. Gases in the atmosphere hold in heat around Earth, creating the _____.

What Causes Climate Change?

16. Changes in the amount of energy the Sun sends out may be related to _____.

17. Ocean currents help move Earth's heat, carrying heat from the _____ to the _____.

18. Dust and gas from volcanoes can block _____ and cause cooling.

How Can Climate Affect You?

19. The main health problem in hot climates is _____.

©Macmillan/McGraw-Hill

Climate

This diagram illustrates how different conditions of temperature and precipitation combine to produce many different types of climate. To understand this diagram, first read the labels in large type, which show the main factors in climate. Notice that the diagram is somewhat like a graph, showing how factors interact. Also study the drawings of different types of plants that grow in different climates.

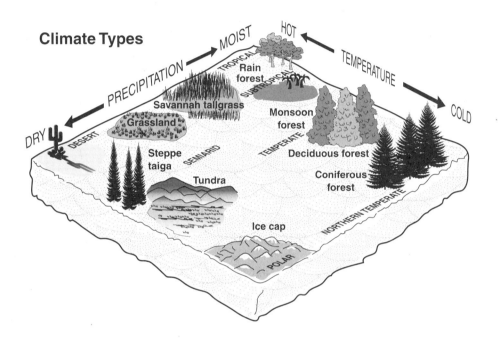

Answer these questions about the diagram above.

1. The lefthand side of the drawing shows the range of _____ from dry to moist.

2. The righthand side of the drawing shows the range of _____ from hot to cold.

3. At the corner with extreme heat and moisture, the climate is _____.

4. Other hot climate types are _____ and _____.

5. What kind of forest is found in a climate that is both cold and moist? _____.

The Greenhouse Effect

This diagram of Earth and its atmosphere illustrates the principle called the greenhouse effect. On the surface of Earth, the diagram pictures some of the sources of greenhouse gases. As with any diagram, start by reading the labels. Also notice the arrows, which show movement in certain directions.

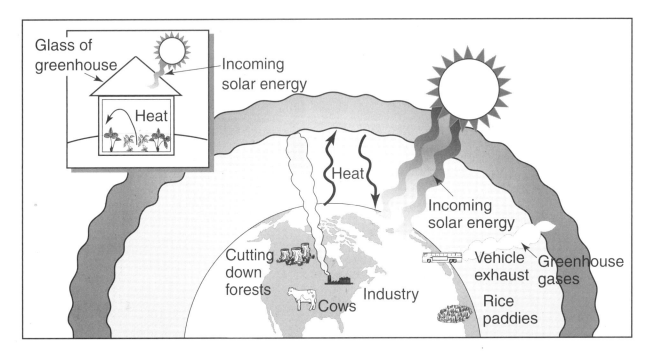

Answer these questions about the diagram above.

1. The source of the heat energy that comes to Earth is _____.

2. When heat radiates off Earth's surface, the _____ bounces it back toward Earth.

3. In industrial nations, industry and _____ are major sources of greenhouse gases.

4. Because green plants take in carbon dioxide, cutting down _____ also increases the amount of greenhouse gases.

5. Use the small inset diagram to explain the term "greenhouse effect."

_____

_____

©Macmillan/McGraw-Hill

Climate

© Macmillan/McGraw-Hill

Vocabulary

temperate

climate

latitude

greenhouse
effect

temperature

equator

radiative
balance

Fill in the blanks.

1. The average weather pattern of a region is
   its _____.

2. The measure of how far north or south of the equator
   something is located is called its _____.

3. It seems that during a sunspot maximum, the
   average _____ of Earth increases slightly.

4. North America is located in the _____
   climate zone.

5. If the amount of energy gained balances the energy lost,
   Earth is in _____.

6. The atmosphere keeps Earth warmer than it would otherwise be because of
   the _____.

7. Ocean currents carry heat away from the _____ and the
   surrounding area.

Answer each question.

8. What information can the plants living in a region tell you about the region's
   climate? Why?

   _____

   _____

   _____

9. Why does an area's closeness to or distance from the ocean help describe that
   area's climate?

   _____

10. How does the atmosphere prevent us from getting too hot during the day?

    _____

    _____

Climate

Vocabulary

| climate | activities | glass | carbon dioxide |
| effect | air | warmer | heat |

Fill in the blanks.

Earth's atmosphere resembles the _____ in a
greenhouse. It lets in sunlight but does not allow _____
to escape. A few gases cause Earth's greenhouse _____.
Water vapor, ozone, and _____ are the main
greenhouse gases. The _____ is made up of only a small
fraction of these gases. Human _____ are responsible
for putting increased amounts of greenhouse gases into the atmosphere.
Earth's _____ might change because of these gases.
Each small increase in these gases causes our planet to become
_____.

Weather Patterns and Climate

Circle the letter of the best answer.

1. Which of these is NOT a factor considered in describing the climate of a region?

   a. distance from the ocean   **b.** the number of mountains nearby

   c. the population of the region   **d.** the amount of precipitation

2. A tornado

   a. has very high air pressure at its center.

   b. has winds less than 75 miles per hour.

   c. always travels in straight lines.

   d. has a very strong updraft at its center.

3. Doppler radar is used to spot

   a. airplanes landing and taking off.   **b.** sunspots.

   c. the spinning movements of clouds.   **d.** coastlines and ship traffic.

4. A storm surge is

   a. a period of heavier rain.

   b. a large swell in the ocean by the shore.

   c. a sudden increase in electrical power to your home.

   d. a crowd of people going to stock up on groceries.

5. Radiative balance with the Sun's heat is maintained by

   a. having 100 cloudy days per year.

   b. the glaciers melting and cooling the ocean.

   c. rain in the tropical climate zones.

   d. Earth radiating heat back into the atmosphere.

6. A hurricane

   a. is formed over warm tropical waters.   **b.** cannot be predicted.

   c. is a storm that follows a narrow path.   **d.** only happens at the shoreline.

©Macmillan/McGraw-Hill

7. During a thunderstorm, you should
   a. phone the shelter for reservations.
   b. go outside and stand under the tallest tree.
   c. go swimming, since you are wet anyway.
   d. stay away from electrical wires and appliances.

8. A cold front occurs when cold air moves
   a. over cold air.
   b. under cold air.
   c. under warm air.
   d. over warm air.

9. Wearing loose clothing on hot days will
   a. make you sweat more.
   b. allow air to cool you.
   c. be very fashionable.
   d. increase your body temperature.

10. Which of these is NOT a gas that contributes to the greenhouse effect?
    a. methane
    b. sulfur dioxide
    c. oxygen
    d. carbon dioxide

11. In a wind blowing from west to east, the point of a wind vane will point
    a. north.
    b. east.
    c. south.
    d. west.

12. The boundary between two air masses with different temperatures is a(n)
    a. isobar.
    b. front.
    c. millibar.
    d. occluded front.

13. Thunderstorms form in
    a. cumulonimbus clouds.
    b. cirronimbulus clouds.
    c. cumulus clouds.
    d. cirrus clouds.

14. Which kind of air mass has cold, dry air?
    a. Maritime Polar
    b. Continental Polar
    c. Maritime Tropical
    d. Continental Tropical

© Macmillan/McGraw-Hill

● # Name That Word

Read each description, then write the word or words being described. Use the
Word Box to check your spelling.

Word Box				
front	storm surge	cirrus cloud	thunderstorm	air pressure
condensation	evaporation	stratus cloud	humidity	Coriolis effect

1. These words identify a cloud that forms in a blanketlike layer.

   _____

2. These words identify a feathery high-altitude cloud made of ice crystals.

   _____

3. This word identifies the changing of gas into a liquid.

   _____

4. This word identifies the changing of liquid into a gas.

   _____

5. This word identifies the amount of water vapor in the air.

   _____

6. These words identify an object's curving movement caused by Earth's rotation.

   _____

7. These words identify the force put on an area by the weight of the air above it.

   _____

8. This word identifies a boundary between air masses with different temperatures.

   _____

9. This word identifies the most common severe storm, formed in cumulonimbus
   clouds. _____

10. These words identify a great rise of the sea along a shore caused by
    low-pressure clouds. _____

Crossword

Read each clue. Write the answer.

Across

1. Change from a gas to a liquid
2. Weather map line connecting places with equal pressure
3. Pellets of ice
5. Layers of gas surrounding Earth
7. Opposite of cool
12. Boundary between air masses of different temperatures
13. Measures air pressure
14. Change from a liquid to a gas

Down

1. A region's average weather pattern
4. Large area in the atmosphere where the air has similar properties
6. Amount of water vapor in the air
8. Funnel-shaped wind storm
9. Moving air
10. What the lower atmosphere is like at a given time
11. A cloud at ground level

©Macmillan/McGraw-Hill

Crack-a-Code

Code Key

A B C D E F G H I J K L M N O P Q R S T U V W X Y Z

**Use the Code Key to help you decode each word.
Then draw a line to its meaning.**

1. _____   a. the amount of water vapor in the air

2. _____   b. average weather in a region

3. _____   c. device to measure wind speed

4. _____   d. cumulonimbus cloud in which a
                                             thunderstorm forms

5. _____   e. weather map line connecting places
                                             with equal air pressure

6. _____   f. what the lower atmosphere is like at a
                                             given place and time

7. _____   g. pellets of ice

Chapter
Graphic
Organizer
Chapter 10

Properties and Structure of Matter

You can use a spider map to organize the main ideas and supporting details of a topic such as properties of matter. Look at the example shown below. The central oval contains the topic being studied. Each branch extending from the oval represents a main idea of the topic. Each branch extending from one of the main ideas represents a supporting detail.

Example

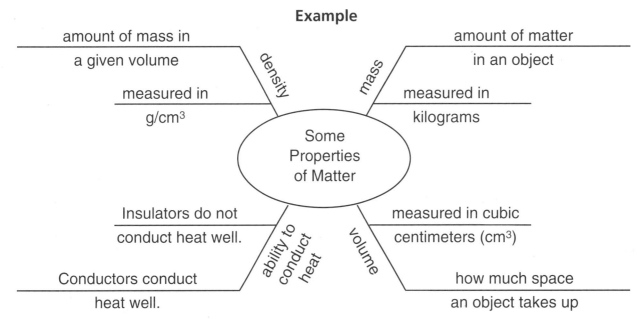

amount of mass in a given volume

measured in g/cm³

density

mass

amount of matter in an object

measured in kilograms

Some Properties of Matter

Insulators do not conduct heat well.

Conductors conduct heat well.

ability to conduct heat

volume

measured in cubic centimeters (cm³)

how much space an object takes up

Complete the spider diagram below for the topic What Matter Is Made Of. The main ideas have already been filled in for you.

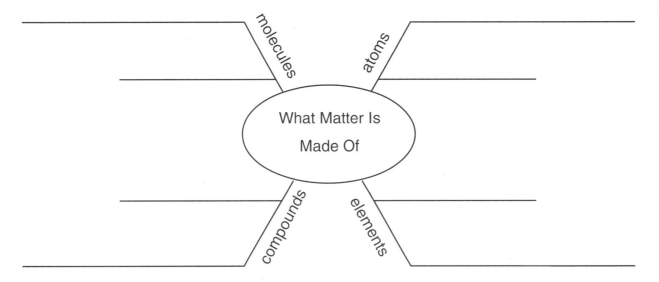

molecules

atoms

What Matter Is Made Of

compounds

elements

Chapter Reading Skill
Chapter 10

Main Idea and Supporting Details

The main idea tells what a story's about. Other sentences contain details that support, or tell more about, the main idea.

Read the following paragraphs, based on information from this chapter of your textbook. **Circle the main idea and underline the supporting details.**

1. What makes things sink or float? It all depends on density, or how much matter an object has for its size. The object's mass divided by its volume gives us its density. If the object's density is less than water's density, the object floats in water. If the object's density is greater than water's density, the object sinks.

2. Atoms contain three kinds of particles—protons, neutrons, and electrons. The protons and neutrons are in the nucleus, the atom's very dense center. The electrons are outside the nucleus. Electrons have about 2,000 times less mass than protons or neutrons. Protons carry one positive electric charge, electrons carry one negative electric charge, and neutrons have no charge at all!

Now reread the Science Magazine article "Animals: Icy Survival." **Then write the main idea of the article, and list at least four supporting details.**

Main Idea: _____

_____

Supporting Details:

1. _____

2. _____

3. _____

4. _____

© Macmillan/McGraw - Hill

The Very Idea!

Read the following paragraphs, based on information in this chapter of your textbook. One paragraph is based on the Science Magazine article "Animals: Icy Survival." **After reading the paragraphs, write the main idea of each and list some of the supporting details.**

1. Dewdrops are not raindrops. Where do the dewdrops on a flower come from? They are water from the air around the flower! In the air the water was a gas, or vapor. When the surface of the flower became cold enough, the water vapor near the flower condensed. It became liquid water. The condensed water formed dewdrops on the petals of the flower.

Main Idea:

_____

_____

Supporting Details:

_____

_____

_____

_____

2. Why does ice float? Doesn't water become denser when it turns to ice? To answer that, you have to look at what happens to water molecules when they get cold enough to freeze. As water freezes, its molecules are kept farther apart than when water is liquid. Ice is only nine-tenths as dense as liquid water, so when water freezes, it expands. That's why ice floats!

Main Idea:

_____

_____

Supporting Details:

_____

_____

_____

_____

Physical Properties

Fill in the blanks. Reading Skill: **Main Idea and Supporting Details** - questions 13, 18

What Is Matter?

1. A measure of the amount of matter in an object is _____.

2. A(n) _____ measures mass.

3. Mass is often measured in _____.

4. A measure of how much space a sample of matter takes up is _____.

5. Anything that has mass and takes up space is _____.

6. The _____ of an object is a measure of the force of gravity between Earth and the object.

7. An object's _____ is a measure of the amount of matter in the object compared to known masses.

8. Scientists use a quantity called the _____ to measure force.

9. An object's weight depends on its _____ in the universe.

What Is Density?

10. The _____ of an object tells us how massive something is for its size.

11. As long as conditions such as _____ do not change, the density of a substance does not change.

12. Each _____ has its own density.

How Dense Are Solids, Liquids and Gases?

13. A measure of how tightly packed matter is is called _____.

14. As more matter gets packed into the same amount of space, the material's density _____.

© Macmillan/McGraw-Hill

How Does Density Make Things Sink or Float?

15. Air is much less dense than water, so a beachball _____.

16. An object's ability to float is called its _____.

17. Objects have enough buoyancy to float when they are less _____ than the liquid in which they are placed.

What Are Conductors and Insulators?

18. When materials _____ energy well, they allow energy to flow through them easily.

19. When materials _____ against the passage of energy, they do not readily permit energy to flow.

20. Metals like copper are good _____ of electricity.

What Is Magnetism?

21. A(n) _____ has north and south poles.

22. Opposite poles _____ one another.

How Do We Use Properties of Matter?

23. Engineers and scientists use _____ of matter when they design and build things.

24. Materials with very low density and relatively great strength, called _____, are very good insulators against heat.

What Is Matter?

These two drawings compare mass and weight on Earth and on the Moon. Think about what is happening to the astronaut each time. Note what is being measured, how it is measured, and what units are used.

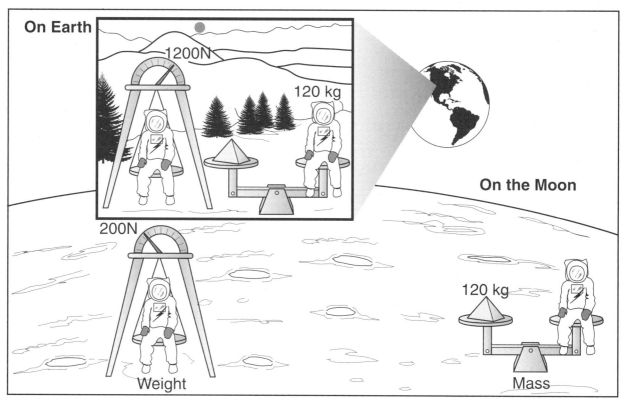

Answer these questions about the diagram above.

1. What is being measured by the pan scale in each drawing? What unit is used?

_____

2. What is being measured on the double-pan balance? What unit is used?

_____

3. What happens to the weight of the astronaut on the Moon?

_____

4. What happens to the mass of the astronaut on the Moon?

_____

5. What number should be on the mass on the double-pan balance on Earth?

_____

How Dense Are Solids, Liquids, and Gases?

These drawings show three different states of matter, using water as an example. The boxes show how the water particles are arranged and how they move. Note how the particles differ from box to box. Make sure you know which box goes with each state of matter.

Gas (steam)

Solid
(ice)

Liquid
(water)

Answer these questions about the diagram above.

1. Which particles are the most orderly? _____

2. Which particles are moving the most? _____

3. Which particles are close together but can slide around each other?

   _____

©Macmillan/McGraw-Hill

Physical Properties

Match the correct letter with the description.

_____ 1. to allow energy or electricity to flow through readily

_____ 2. a measure of the force of gravity between Earth and an object

_____ 3. matter in which particles line up pole to pole

_____ 4. the amount of space an object takes up

_____ 5. all of the gases, liquids, and solids in the world

_____ 6. the amount of matter in an object

_____ 7. not to allow energy to flow through readily

_____ 8. tells us how massive something is for its size

Vocabulary

a. mass

b. volume

c. weight

d. density

e. magnetic

f. conduct

g. insulate

h. matter

Use the terms above to identify the property used.

9. use a flashlight _____

10. use a compass _____

11. use a paperweight _____

12. sink marbles in the bottom of a fish bowl _____

13. drink 8 ounces of water _____

14. wear layers during the winter _____

15. step on a scale _____

© Macmillan/McGraw-Hill

Physical Properties

Vocabulary

conduct	measure	insulate
dense	float	metal
handles	mass	
volume	properties	

Fill in the blanks.

To tell one type of matter in objects from another you can

_____ their _____. The amount of matter in

an object is its _____. The amount of space it takes up is its

_____. If one liquid is less _____ than another

it will _____ on top of it. Materials that _____

energy allow it to flow through readily. Cooking pans are made of

_____ since it lets heat pass through. However, the

_____ are made of wood or ceramic so your hands don't get

burned. These materials _____ against the passage of energy.

Elements and Compounds

Fill in the blanks. Reading Skill: **Main Idea and Supporting Details** - questions 1, 14

What Is Matter Made Of?

1. The basic building blocks of all matter are _____.

2. Elements are pure substances that _____ be broken down into simpler substances.

What Are Compounds?

3. Any substance that is formed by the _____ of two or more elements is called a compound.

4. Compounds can only be broken apart by _____.

5. Compounds have _____ properties than the elements that make them up.

How Do You Write a Compound's Name?

6. Scientists write symbols for compounds called _____.

7. A formula contains numbers below the elements called _____.

8. The subscripts in chemical formulas tell us the _____ of particles that combine in a compound.

What Are Elements Made Of?

9. A(n) _____ is the smallest unit of an element that retains the properties of the element.

What Is Inside Atoms?

10. The three kinds of particles that atoms contain are _____ _____ and _____.

11. The tiny, very dense body in the atom's center is called the atomic _____.

12. The number of _____ in an atom determines what element it is.

©Macmillan/McGraw-Hill

What Properties Do Elements Have?

13. We now know of _____ elements.

14. Some elements take part in chemical _____ much more easily than others.

15. About three-fourths of the elements are _____.

16. Properties of metals include:

    a. _____,

    b. _____, and

    c. _____.

How Can the Elements Be Grouped?

17. In 1869, Mendeleyev found that the properties of the elements went through _____.

18. The groups in Mendeleyev's table contained elements with similar _____ properties.

19. We call Mendeleyev's table the periodic table after the periodic changes found in the elements' _____.

What Are Molecules?

20. Particles that contain more than one atom joined together are called _____.

21. Molecules of _____ always contain only one kind of atom.

22. _____ are made up of molecules that have different kinds of atoms joined together.

23. When a compound forms from elements, changes occur in the way that the atoms are _____.

How Do We Use Compounds?

24. Petroleum is a complex mixture of _____.

25. _____ comes from petroleum.

©Macmillan/McGraw-Hill

What Is Inside Atoms?

These three pictures show three very common atoms: hydrogen, helium, and carbon. Note how each proton, neutron, and electron is represented. Then count the number of each kind of these particles in each atom.

○ — electron

● — proton

● — neutron

Atoms are made of protons, neutrons, and electrons. The number of protons an atom has determines what element it is.

Hydrogen

Helium

Carbon

Answer these questions about the diagram above.

1. Which two particles are found in each of the atoms?

   _____

2. Which particle is NOT found in Hydrogen? _____

3. Which particle is NOT found in the nucleus? _____

4. Which atom weighs the most? Why?

   _____

What Are Molecules?

These pictures show different elements and compounds. Compare the picture of each with the formula below it.

Elements

Nitrogen
N_2

Oxygen
O_2 and O_3

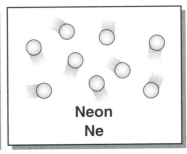

Neon
Ne

Compounds

Carbon dioxide
CO_2

Water
H_2O

Methane
CH_4
(natural gas)

Answer these questions about the pictures above.

1. Which of these pictures show molecules?

_____

2. What kinds of atoms make up these molecules?

_____

3. What is the ratio of the number of oxygen atoms to the number of carbon atoms in the carbon dioxide molecule? _____

4. How are the elements nitrogen and oxygen different from neon?

_____

_____

5. How do the pictures compare to the chemical formulas?

_____

Elements and Compounds

Match the correct letter with the description.

_____ 1. the dense center part of an atom

_____ 2. a chemical combination of two or more elements into a single substance

_____ 3. the smallest unit of an element that still has the properties of the element

_____ 4. contains the symbols for the elements that make it up

_____ 5. an uncharged particle in the nucleus of an atom

_____ 6. a particle that contains more than one atom joined together

_____ 7. a basic building block of matter

_____ 8. a particle with a negative charge moving around the nucleus of an atom

_____ 9. one or two letters that identify an element

_____ 10. a particle with a positive charge in the nucleus of an atom

Vocabulary

a. element
b. compound
c. atom
d. proton
e. neutron
f. electron
g. nucleus
h. molecule
i. chemical formula
j. symbol

Answer each question.

11. Which elements are poor conductors of electricity? _____

_____

12. On the periodic table, where can you find the metalloids?

_____

13. What is the difference between an atom and a molecule?

_____

_____

Elements and Compounds

Vocabulary

electron	compound	elements
symbol	properties	atom
table	neutron	proton

Fill in the blanks.

Scientists have identified 112 _____. The smallest unit of each
of these pure substances that has its properties is a(n) _____.
These units are made of smaller particles. The _____ has a
negative charge, the _____ has a positive charge, and the
_____ has no charge. Each substance is given a special
_____ of one or two letters. A scientist named Dmitri
Mendeleyev created a periodic _____. He grouped the substances according to chemical _____. Two or more substances
can combine chemically to form a new _____.

Name_____ **Date**_____

Lesson Outline
Lesson 3

Solids, Liquids, and Gases

Fill in the blanks. Reading Skill: **Main Idea and Supporting Details** - questions 2, 4, 6, 14, 15, 16

What Are the States of Matter?

1. When water absorbs enough heat, it turns into a(n) _____ called steam.

2. The three states of matter are:

   a. _____,

   b. _____, and

   c. _____.

3. When a change of _____ occurs, the identity of the substance stays the same.

4. Substances change state because their _____ are arranged in a different way.

5. The molecules of any substance are _____ to each other.

6. Adding or removing _____ makes substances change from one state to another.

7. When molecules are linked in organized positions, a(n) _____ results.

8. When heat is absorbed by a solid, the molecules vibrate _____.

9. Heat causes the molecules of a solid to _____ from each other, making the solid become a liquid.

10. Every substance has its own particular melting point and _____.

11. When a substance is melting or boiling, its _____ stays the same.

12. When heat is removed from a boiling substance, it _____.

13. The melting point is also called the _____ point.

© Macmillan/McGraw-Hill

How Can Matter Change to a Gas?

14. When a liquid _____, it gradually changes to a gas.

15. When a liquid _____, it changes to a gas rapidly.

16. Once all the liquid becomes steam, the _____ goes up.

What Are the Properties of Solids, Liquids, and Gases?

17. Solids keep their _____.

18. _____ take the shape of their containers.

19. Gases fill the _____ of their containers.

20. When the temperature of a material increases, its particles move
    _____.

21. Materials _____ as they get hotter.

22. Materials _____ as the get cooler.

23. Substances that are _____ expand or contract the most with
    changing temperature.

How Can Expansion and Contraction Be Used?

24. The liquid in a _____ expands or contracts with changes
    in temperature.

What Are the States of Matter?

This diagram shows what happens to particles during changes of state. This is not what you would actually see, but the diagram helps you understand what is actually happening. Focus on how much the particles move.

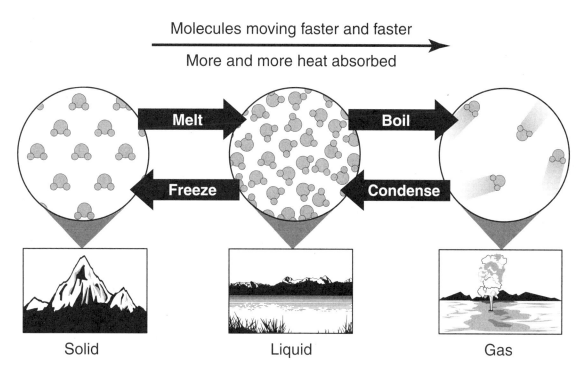

Molecules moving faster and faster

More and more heat absorbed

Melt Boil

Freeze Condense

Solid   Liquid   Gas

Answer these questions about the diagram above.

1. What happens to the speed of molecules as they absorb heat?

_____

2. In which state have the particles absorbed the most heat? _____

3. Which particles show the least amount of motion? _____

4. In which state do the particles occupy the greatest amount of space?

_____

What Are the States of Matter?

This line graph shows the change in temperature of water and PDCB over time. To get the data, a sample of each is heated and its temperature at each time interval is recorded. As you study a graph, note the title, the two axes, and the general shape of the lines.

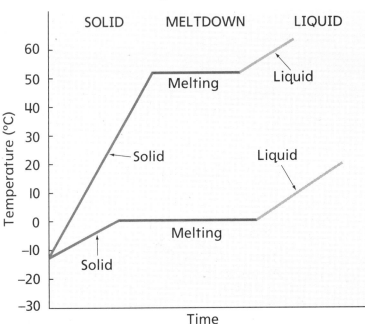

Melting of PDCB and Water

Answer these questions about the diagram above.

1. If water has a melting point of 0°C, which line shows the data for water?

_____

2. What is the melting point of PDCB? _____

3. Why does the water line flatten out after 0°C?

_____

4. What do you think is happening during the time the temperature is not increasing? _____

5. What state of matter is the PDCB in until 52°C? _____

© Macmillan/McGraw-Hill

Solids, Liquids, and Gases

Match the correct letter with the description.

_____ 1. the temperature at which a liquid changes state into a solid

_____ 2. the temperature at which a solid changes state into a liquid

_____ 3. a liquid slowly changing into a gas

_____ 4. any of the forms matter can exist in

_____ 5. a gas turning to a liquid

_____ 6. the temperature at which a liquid changes state into a gas

_____ 7. the temperature stays constant during this even though heat is being added or removed

_____ 8. cooling causes particles to get closer together and materials do this

_____ 9. materials spread out as they get hotter

Vocabulary

a. state of matter
b. melting point
c. boiling point
d. freezing point
e. evaporation
f. condensation
g. change of state
h. expand
i. contract

10. Explain why the temperature of water stays the same for a while once it starts boiling.

_____

_____

11. Name one way you benefit from each of the following states of matter.

solid _____

liquid _____

gas _____

12. How are boiling and evaporation the same? How are they different?

_____

_____

_____

Solids, Liquids, and Gases

Vocabulary

solid	expand	evaporation
freezing	properties	liquid
gas	states	
molecules	contract	

Fill in the blanks.

Most substances exist in one of three _____ of matter.

Whenever a change occurs, the substance gains new _____.

This happens because the _____ are arranged differently.

Each pure substance has a melting point, or temperature at which a(n)

_____ changes into a(n) _____. Each also has

a boiling point at which the liquid changes into a(n) _____.

The process by which a liquid slowly turns into a gas is known as

_____. The temperature at which a liquid changes into

a solid is known as the _____ point. Most materials

_____, or become smaller, as they get cooler. They

_____, or become larger, as they get hotter.

Properties and Structure of Matter

Circle the letter of the best answer.

1. A particle outside the nucleus of an atom is a(n)
   a. proton.
   b. electron.
   c. insulate.
   d. molecule.

2. The amount of space an object takes up is its
   a. density.
   b. mass.
   c. volume.
   d. weight.

3. A material that does not readily permit heat to flow through it is a material that
   a. insulates.
   b. conducts.
   c. measures.
   d. weighs.

4. The amount of mass contained in a given volume is its
   a. buoyancy.
   b. density.
   c. insulation.
   d. weight.

5. A measure of the force of gravity between Earth and an object is its
   a. density.
   b. mass.
   c. volume.
   d. weight.

6. The amount of matter in an object is called its
   a. density.
   b. mass.
   c. volume.
   d. weight.

7. A charged particle in the nucleus of the atom is a(n)
   a. electron.
   b. molecule.
   c. proton.
   d. neutron.

© Macmillan/McGraw-Hill

8. A chemical combination of two or more elements into a single substance is a(n)

   a. compound.   b. metal.

   c. molecule.   d. nucleus.

9. A group of more than one atom joined together that acts like a single particle is a(n)

   a. neutron.   b. metal.

   c. molecule.   d. nucleus.

10. A pure substance that cannot be broken down into anything simpler is a(n)

    a. compound.   b. element.

    c. molecule.   d. nucleus.

11. The smallest unit of an element that still has the properties of the element is a(n)

    a. atom.   b. compound.

    c. molecule.   d. nucleus.

12. The dense center part of an atom is its

    a. molecule.   b. neutron.

    c. nucleus.   d. proton.

13. Any of the forms matter can exist in is what is called a(n)

    a. change of matter.   b. molecule.

    c. periodic.   d. state of matter.

14. Each different substance has its own boiling temperature called the

    a. melting point.   b. freezing point.

    c. liquefying point.   d. boiling point.

© Macmillan/McGraw-Hill

Chapter Summary

1. What is the name of the chapter you just finished reading?

   _____

   _____

2. What are four vocabulary words you learned in the chapter?
   Write a definition for each.

   _____

   _____

   _____

   _____

   _____

   _____

   _____

   _____

3. What are two main ideas that you learned in this chapter?

   _____

   _____

   _____

   _____

   _____

   _____

©Macmillan/McGraw-Hill

Forms of Matter and Energy

You can use a diagram, like the one below about the movement of heat, to show how one or more events may cause another event to happen. Each arrow points from a cause to an effect. Notice that the effect in this diagram can be caused by three different events.

Movement of Heat

Cause   Effect

conduction

convection   The temperature of the warmer object decreases, and the temperature of the cooler object increases.

radiation

Complete the cause-and-effect diagram shown below. This diagram involves the separation of a mixture of sand, salt, and iron filings. Notice that each effect in this diagram has only one cause.

Separation of a Mixture

Cause   Effect

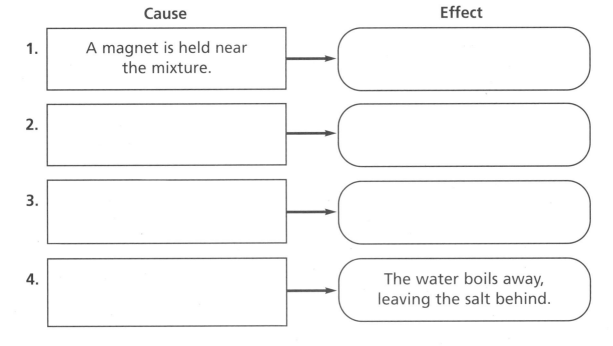

1. A magnet is held near the mixture.

2.

3.

4.   The water boils away, leaving the salt behind.

©Macmillan/McGraw-Hill

Cause and Effect

Often there's more than one cause for an effect. For example, you toss a toy bone for your dog to catch. The dog jumps, but misses the toy, and bumps into your mom's favorite potted plant. The plant falls over, and mud spills all over the rug! You, your dog, and the toy bone are all causes of the mess . . . but only you can clean it up!

Read each cause below. Write two possible effects.

1. Our school bus had a flat tire . . .

   _____

   _____

2. Jamie forgot to set his alarm . . .

   _____

   _____

3. All the fifth graders in our school took the test . . .

   _____

   _____

4. Carmen found a CD player that someone left in the park . . .

   _____

   _____

5. Brian forgot to lock the front door when he came home . . .

   _____

   _____

6. Alex and Andy saved their allowances all year . . .

   _____

   _____

© Macmillan/McGraw-Hill

If . . . Then Fun

Look at the drawing below. Then read each **If . . . then** statement and follow directions.

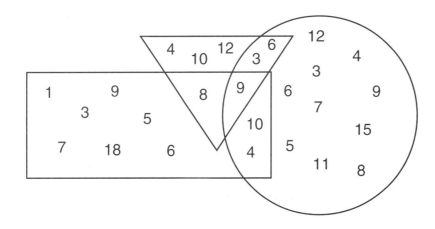

1. **If** the numbers are in the triangle **only, then** add them.

2. **If** the numbers are in the circle **only, then** add them.

3. **If** the numbers are in the rectangle **only, then** add them.

4. **If** the numbers are in the triangle **and** rectangle **only, then** add them.

5. **If** the numbers are in the triangle **and** circle **only, then** add them.

6. **If** the numbers are in the rectangle **and** circle **only, then** add them.

7. **If** the numbers are in the triangle, circle, **and** rectangle, **then** add them.

8. **If** there are numbers in boxes 1 through 7, **then** add them together.

9. **If** the answer in box 8 is 192 or more, **then** write a 5 in this box.

©Macmillan/McGraw-Hill

Mixtures and Solutions

Fill in the blanks. Reading Skill: **Cause and Effect** - questions 5, 11, 16, 17

What Is a Mixture?

1. Materials that are physically combined form _____.

2. Materials that are chemically combined form _____.

3. In mixtures, the parts keep their original _____.

4. A compound has _____ properties from the substances that combine to make it.

How Can Mixtures Be Classified?

5. If the substances in a mixture blend completely, we call this a(n) _____.

6. _____ have properties in between those of solutions and heterogeneous mixtures.

What Kinds of Solutions Are There?

7. Solutions never settle into _____.

8. The substance that makes up the smaller part of a solution is called the _____.

9. The substance that makes up the larger amount of the solution is the _____.

What Is Solubility?

10. Solubility explains the ability of a solute to _____ in a solvent.

11. Some substances do not dissolve in others; when this happens, we say they are _____.

12. You can separate alcohol and water by _____ them.

What Are Heterogeneous Mixtures Like?

13. Rocks are examples of _____ mixtures.

14. Heterogeneous mixtures can settle into _____.

15. _____ form when one substance is insoluble, or does not dissolve in a solvent.

What Types of Colloids Are There?

16. Milk is an example of a(n) _____.

17. _____ have either liquid drops or solid particles spread through a gas.

How Can Mixtures Be Separated?

18. A(n) _____ separation gets the parts of a mixture away without changing their identities.

19. To separate sand and wood chips, first pour in _____.

Which Resources Come from Mixtures?

20. Seawater is a mixture that can be used as a(n) _____ for fresh water.

21. Crude oil, our major _____ source, is a mixture, too.

© Macmillan/McGraw-Hill

How Can Mixtures Be Separated?

These drawings show someone separating a mixture of salt and sand. Note what is happening in each step and think about the processes that are going on.

1. To separate a mixture of sand and salt, pour in water and stir. The salt dissolves, but the sand doesn't.

2. Use a filter to separate the sand from the salt water.

3. Then let the water evaporate to get back the salt.

Answer these questions about the diagram above.

1. What will happen after water is added to the salt and sand mixture?

_____

2. In the second picture, what does the filter paper keep out of the second beaker? _____

3. What will you find in the bottom of the second beaker in the second drawing?

_____

4. In the third picture, what is leaving the beaker? _____

5. What is left behind in the beaker in the third picture? _____

Separating Alcohol and Water

This diagram shows a distillation apparatus that is separating a mixture of water and alcohol. The alcohol has a lower boiling point and escapes the liquid mixture faster than the water. As you study the diagram, start on the left and trace the process. Think about what is happening in each part of the diagram.

You could separate alcohol and water by heating them in this apparatus.

The vapors cool and condense.

Vapor

Thermometer

Cold water

Waste water

Alcohol and water mixture

Alcohol and water are heated. Alcohol boils at a lower temperature than water, so at the beginning, more of the vapor will be alcohol than water.

The condensed liquid has more alcohol than water.

Answer these questions about the diagram above.

1. What is happening in the flask on the left?

   _____

2. Where do you think the gas particles in the tube above the flask came from? Why? _____

3. What is happening in the middle of the long tube?

   _____

4. What liquid would you expect to find in the flask on the right?

   _____

Mixtures and Solutions

Match the correct letter with the description.

_____ 1. a liquid spread through another liquid

_____ 2. a mixture of substances that settle into layers in a fluid

_____ 3. two or more parts blended together yet keeping their own properties and not turning into a new substance

_____ 4. This kind of change results in a mixture.

_____ 5. a solid spread through a liquid

_____ 6. liquid drops or solid particles spread through a gas

_____ 7. This forms when one substance is insoluble, or does not dissolve in a solvent.

_____ 8. a mixture in which substances are completely blended so that the properties are the same throughout and the substances stay blended

_____ 9. particles (or droplets) large enough to block out light spread throughout another substance

_____ 10. This kind of combining results in a new substance.

_____ 11. a gas spread through a liquid or solid

Vocabulary

a. mixture
b. solution
c. suspension
d. colloid
e. emulsion
f. aerosol
g. gel
h. foam
i. chemical
j. physical
k. heterogeneous

Use the terms above to describe the mixtures below. Then write if they are easy or hard to separate.

12. air   _____   _____

13. a jar of coins   _____   _____

14. a rock   _____   _____

15. gelatin dessert _____   _____

16. whipped cream _____   _____

17. Give an example of how an aerosol is used, how a foam is used.

_____

_____

Mixtures and Solutions

Vocabulary

solution	heterogeneous	emulsions	properties
suspensions	colloid	homogeneous	separate

Fill in the blanks.

A mixture is the physical combination of two or more substances. The substances in a mixture keep their own _____ without forming new substances. In a _____, the substances are blended completely. The mixture looks the same everywhere, or is _____. In _____ mixtures, the substances may be only partly blended. Examples of heterogeneous mixtures are _____. They _____ into layers when they are left alone. A third type of mixture, _____, has properties in between those of solutions and heterogeneous mixtures. There are many types of colloids, such as _____, aerosols, foams, and gels.

©Macmillan/McGraw-Hill

Chemical Changes

Fill in the blanks. Reading Skill: **Cause and Effect** - questions 3, 7, 10, 12, 14, 15

What Are Physical and Chemical Changes?

1. In a(n) _____ change, matter changes in size, shape, or state without changing identity.

2. Chemical changes occur when _____ link together in new ways.

3. A change in matter that produces a new compound with different properties from the original is a(n) _____.

4. A chemical _____ is a chemical change of original substances into one or more new substances.

5. A(n) _____ is one of the original substances before a chemical change.

6. The new substances produced by a chemical reaction are called _____.

7. In the reaction between baking soda and vinegar, the baking soda and vinegar are the reactants, and _____, water, and sodium acetate are the products.

What Are the Signs of a Chemical Change?

8. Signs that a chemical change has occurred include:

   a. a(n) _____ change,

   b. formation of a(n) _____, and the formation of light and

   c. _____.

©Macmillan/McGraw-Hill

9. When blueberry juice is mixed with a solution of baking soda, it turns a(n) _____ color.

10. The _____ that form when a solution containing dissolved baking soda and lemon juice are mixed indicates that a chemical change has taken place.

11. When you light a match, it gives off _____ and _____.

What Are Some Familiar Chemical Changes?

12. As a cake bakes, a chemical reaction turns the baking soda into sodium carbonate, steam, and _____ gas, causing the cake to rise.

13. The chemical reaction involving baking soda is triggered by _____.

14. The silver sulfide forms when silver reacts with sulfur or _____ in foods or the air.

15. Iron oxide is commonly known as _____.

Which Are Easier to Reverse—Chemical or Physical Changes?

16. Physical changes can sometimes be easily _____.

17. In general chemical changes are _____ to reverse.

© Macmillan/McGraw-Hill

What Are Physical and Chemical Changes?

This diagram shows what happens when baking soda and vinegar are mixed. Note how the atoms are combined into new substances.

Starting substances   New substances

$NaHCO_3$ + CH_3COOH → H_2O + CO_2 + $NaC_2H_3O_2$

Baking soda   Acetic acid   Water + Carbon + Sodium
                  (part of vinegar)   dioxide   acetate

Answer these questions about the diagram above.

1. What elements make up

   Acetic acid?   _____

   Baking soda? _____

2. What happens when the acetic acid and baking soda are mixed?

   _____

   _____

3. What kind of change, physical or chemical, is shown in the picture? How do you know?

   _____

   _____

4. What do you notice about the total number of atoms before and after the chemicals are mixed?

   _____

© Macmillan/McGraw-Hill

Which Are Easier to Reverse–Chemical or Physical Changes?

These drawings show changes that you may have seen at home. Think about how these changes happen. Also remember the differences between physical and chemical changes.

Answer these questions about the drawings above.

1. Is burning toast a physical or chemical change? How do you know?

_____

_____

2. What kind of physical change can you see when a candle burns? How can you tell it is a physical change?

_____

_____

3. What kind of chemical change can you see when a candle burns? How can you tell it is a chemical change?

_____

_____

Chemical Changes

Match the correct letter with the description.

_____ 1. one of the new substances produced when a chemical reaction takes place

_____ 2. a change in size, shape, or state, without forming a new substance

_____ 3. a chemical change of original substance(s) into one or more new substances

_____ 4. one of the original substance(s) before a chemical reaction takes place

_____ 5. a change in matter that produces a new substance with different properties from the original

Vocabulary

a. physical change

b. chemical change

c. chemical reaction

d. reactant

e. product

Identify the following as "chemical" or "physical."

6. a change in size not the substance _____

7. produces heat _____

8. a change in shape not the substance _____

9. produces a gas not originally present _____

10. change of state _____

11. produces a new color from a new substance _____

12. tarnish _____

13. baking a cake _____

14. burning a candle _____

Chemical Changes

Vocabulary

chemical reaction	products	rust	physical
mixture	reactants	chemical change	

Fill in the blanks.

In a _____ change, matter may change its size, its shape, or

its _____ without also changing identity. When atoms link

together to form new substances, a _____ takes place.

The _____ are the original substances. New substances

produced when a _____ takes place are called the

_____. A common example of this kind of change is

_____ or iron oxide.

Acids and Bases

Fill in the blanks. 📖 Reading Skill: **Cause and Effect** - questions 1, 2, 6, 7, 9, 12, 16, 18

What Are Acids and Bases?

1. A(n) _____ tastes sour and turns blue litmus paper red.

2. Ammonia and baking soda, which are _____, taste bitter and turn red litmus paper blue.

3. Acids give away hydrogen particles, or _____ ions in a reaction.

4. Particles that are made up of one oxygen and one hydrogen atom linked together are called _____ ions.

5. Water is neither acidic nor basic and is therefore _____.

How Can You Tell if Something Is an Acid or a Base?

6. A(n) _____ is a substance that changes color when it is mixed with an acid or a base.

7. _____, a common vegetable indicator, is colorless in acid and turns pink in a base.

How Can Indicators Be Useful?

8. A test kit has paper strips that are soaked with an indicator to reveal how _____ the soil is.

9. Aquarium owners or pond owners periodically have to check how acidic the _____ is to make sure it is healthy for the fish and plants.

© Macmillan/McGraw-Hill

Are All Acids and Bases the Same?

10. The strength of an acid is its _____.

11. The strength of a base is its _____.

12. Acidity and alkalinity depend on how many hydronium and hydroxide _____ there are in a solution.

13. Soren Sorenson developed the _____ scale in 1909 to compare acidic and basic solutions.

14. A pH of _____ means that there are a lot of hydronium ions in the solution, and the solution is very acidic.

15. A pH of _____ means that there are a lot of hydroxide ions in a solution, and that the solution is very basic.

16. pH _____ changes to a different color depending on the exact pH of a solution.

How Can Acids and Bases Be Used?

17. Many _____, like tomatoes, grapefruit, lemons, and limes, get their flavor from acids.

18. _____ help to increase the pH of your stomach back to its normal level.

What Are Acids and Bases?

The pictures below show models of a hydronium ion (H^+) and a hydroxide ion (OH^-). Acids give off hydronium ions and bases give off hydroxide ions. A substance which give off neither of these ions is neutral.

Hydronium ion

Hydroxide ion

Answer the following questions about the picture above.

1. Which ion contains oxygen?

   _____

   _____

2. If a solution gives off neither hydronium nor hydroxide ions, what does that indicate?

   _____

   _____

© Macmillan/McGraw-Hill

Are All Acids and Bases the Same?

The picture below shows a pH scale. The scale goes from 1, the most acidic, to 14, the most basic. pH 7 indicates a neutral substance on the scale.

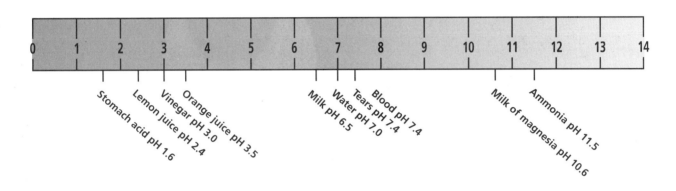

Answer the following questions about the picture above.

1. Which substance is more acidic—lemon juice or orange juice?

   _____

2. Which of the following would help to counteract stomach acids better— vinegar or milk?

   _____

3. Which solution is neutral?

   _____

Acids and Bases

Fill in the blanks.

Vocabulary

a. acidity

b. acids

c. pH

d. indicator

e. alkalinity

f. neutral

g. hydronium

h. bases

1. Acidity and _____ depend on how many hydronium and hydroxide ions are in a solution.

2. _____ taste bitter and turn red litmus paper blue.

3. _____ and hydroxide ions combine to make water.

4. Litmus paper is an example of a(n) _____ because its color changes when it is mixed with an acid or a base.

5. The strength of an acid is called its _____.

6. A solution that is neither acidic nor basic, such as water, is a(n) _____ substance.

7. The _____ of a solution is a measure of the solution's acidity or alkalinity.

8. _____ give off hydrogen particles or hydronium ions.

Answer each question.

9. Describe how red cabbage juice can be used as an indicator.

_____

_____

_____

10. Who developed the pH scale and how is it used to describe acids and bases?

_____

_____

_____

Acids and Bases

Vocabulary

neutral	bases	strength	alkalinity
acid	indicator	hydronium	hydroxide

Fill in the blanks.

In a reaction, acids give off particles called _____ ions.

_____ give off _____ ions that are made up

of one oxygen and one hydrogen atom linked together. A substance that is

_____ does not release either hydronium or hydroxide ions.

You can make a(n) _____ neutral by mixing it with a base.

A(n) _____, such as litmus paper, changes color when it is

mixed with an acid or a base. An indicator can be used to measure the

_____ of an acid or its acidity. Acidity and _____,

the strength of a base, depend on how many hydronium and hydroxide ions

are in a solution.

Matter and Energy

Fill in the blanks. 📖 Reading Skill: **Cause and Effect** - questions 1, 12

What Is Electrical Energy?

1. A battery provides _____ energy.

2. The chemical reactions in a battery produce _____, each of which carries energy.

3. When a battery is connected to a light bulb with wires, a(n) _____ is formed.

4. When electrons in a circuit pass through a light bulb, they give up some of their energy to the wire in the light bulb, called the _____.

5. The _____ measures amps, telling us how many electrons flow each second.

6. The _____ measures volts.

What Are Other Forms of Energy?

7. Energy is a measure of how much _____ something can produce.

8. Work is using _____ to move an object.

9. Energy is not a type of _____.

10. Any object that is moving has _____ energy.

11. Stored energy is referred to as _____ energy.

©Macmillan/McGraw-Hill

How Can We Describe Thermal Energy?

12. The transfer of thermal energy from one object to another is

_____.

13. Heat always flows from _____ materials to cooler materials, never the other way.

How Does Heat Move?

14. In _____, thermal energy flows through objects without the movement of any matter.

15. In _____ hot parts of a material rise while cooler parts sink.

16. Heat is transferred through electromagnetic rays in _____.

What Materials Conduct Heat Well?

17. Metals are the best _____ of heat.

18. The molecules in _____ are packed very closely together, and this makes transferring energy easier.

What Is Electrical Energy?

The picture below shows a flow of electrons from a battery through a light bulb's filament. Attaching the positive and negative terminals of the battery to the light bulb creates a closed circuit through which electrons can flow. The flow of electrons causes the filament to give off energy as light and heat.

BATTERY

Flow of Electrons

Hot filament

Answer the following questions about the picture above.

1. How do electrons flow through the circuit?

_____

_____

_____

2. The filament gives off what kinds of energy?

_____

_____

3. Would the light bulb work if you attached both of the battery's terminals to one side of the light bulb? Why?

_____

_____

How Does Heat Move?

These three illustrations show different times during the heating process.
In this case, a piece of metal is being heated. Start at the top and notice how each
picture is different from the one below it.

Heating just started

After a few minutes

After many minutes

Answer these questions about the illustrations above.

1. Which metal particles are the first to react to the heat?

_____

2. How do they react to the heat?

_____

3. How does heat travel down the piece of metal?

_____

_____

©Macmillan/McGraw-Hill

Matter and Energy

Match the correct letter with the description.

_____ 1. the ability to move matter around

_____ 2. when hot parts of a material rise, while cooler parts sink

_____ 3. the energy of a moving object

_____ 4. a thin wire in a bulb

_____ 5. energy stored in an object or material

_____ 6. movement of energy in the form of waves that can travel through empty space

_____ 7. movement of energy from a hot object that comes into contact with a cooler object; the material remains in place

Vocabulary

a. kinetic energy

b. potential energy

c. conduction

d. convection

e. radiation

f. filament

g. energy

Identify the form of energy and write one way you use that kind of energy.

8. carried by light _____

9. stored in links between atoms _____

10. sum of the kinetic and potential energy of a system

_____

11. carried by electrons in circuits _____

12. carried by heat _____

© Macmillan/McGraw-Hill

Matter and Energy

Vocabulary

potential energy	chemical energy	kinetic energy	work
force	matter	forms	

Fill in the blanks.

What is energy? Energy is not a type of _____. It is a measure

of how much _____ something can produce. To scientists, work

means using a _____—a push or a pull—to move an object.

There are many _____ of energy. When something moves, its

energy is called _____. Another main form of energy is

_____. This energy can be described as stored energy. An

example of this is _____, which is the energy stored in

links between atoms.

Forms of Matter and Energy

For each number, circle the letter of the best answer.

1. When a liquid turns blue litmus paper red, this indicates it is a(n)
   - **a.** colloid.
   - **b.** emulsion.
   - **c.** solution.
   - **d.** acid.

2. A mixture in which substances are completely blended so that the properties are the same throughout and the substances stay blended describes a(n)
   - **a.** colloid.
   - **b.** emulsion.
   - **c.** solution.
   - **d.** suspension.

3. When some substance tastes bitter and turns red litmus paper blue, it is a(n)
   - **a.** colloid.
   - **b.** base.
   - **c.** solution.
   - **d.** suspension.

4. A mixture with properties in between those of solutions and heterogeneous mixtures is called a(n)
   - **a.** colloid.
   - **b.** alloy.
   - **c.** indicator.
   - **d.** suspension.

5. Two or more substances blended together that keep their own properties describes a(n)
   - **a.** compound
   - **b.** base.
   - **c.** mixture.
   - **d.** molecule.

6. The strength of a base is called its
   - **a.** alkalinity.
   - **b.** emulsion.
   - **c.** mixture.
   - **d.** solution.

7. When thermal energy flows through objects that are touching, it is called
   - **a.** radiation.
   - **b.** conduction.
   - **c.** convection.
   - **d.** suspension.

© Macmillan/McGraw-Hill

8. A change in matter that produces a new substance with different properties from the original is a
   a. chemical change.   b. kinetic change.
   c. physical change.   d. product change.

9. When something moves, its energy is called
   a. kinetic.   b. potential.
   c. physical.   d. radiation.

10. This is one of the original substances before a chemical reaction takes place.
    a. colloid   b. conductor
    c. product   d. reactant

11. This is one of the new substances produced when a chemical reaction takes place.
    a. colloid   b. conductor
    c. product   d. reactant

12. Energy stored in an object or material is
    a. conduction energy.   b. convection energy.
    c. kinetic energy.   d. potential energy.

13. Movement of energy by the flow of matter from place to place is
    a. conduction.   b. convection.
    c. emulsion.   d. radiation.

14. Movement of energy in the form of waves that can travel through empty space is
    a. conduction.   b. convection.
    c. emulsion.   d. radiation.

● # Choose-a-Word

Circle the word that best completes each sentence.

1. Vinegar, orange juice, and lemon juice are _____.

   bases   **acids**   **neutrals**

2. Pure substances that can't be broken down are called _____.

   compounds   **hydrocarbons**   **elements**

3. The original substances in chemical reactions are called the _____.

   reactants   **products**   **molecules**

4. The _____ of a solution tells how acidic or basic the solution is.

   potential   **indicator**   **pH**

5. An _____ is the smallest unit of an element that still has the properties of that element.

   electron   **atom**   **emulsion**

6. A _____ is formed by two or more elements and acts like a single substance.

   molecule   **colloid**   **compound**

7. If something is _____, it prevents heat from passing through.

   instructed   **insulated**   **radiated**

8. The melting point of a substance is also known as the _____ point.

   boiling   **freezing**   **evaporation**

9. A _____ has properties in between those of solutions and heterogeneous mixtures.

   compound   **suspension**   **colloid**

©Macmillan/McGraw-Hill

Correct-a-Word

Word Box				
potential	emulsion	mass	kinetic	volume
physical	boiling	radiation	gel	

One word in each sentence below is wrong. Cross it out and write the correct word above it. One has been done for you. Use the Word Box to check your spelling.

1. The amount of matter in an object is its ~~density.~~ *mass*

2. The energy of any moving object is kindling energy.

3. The vacuum describes how much space a sample of matter takes up.

4. A gem is a solid spread through a liquid.

5. The melting point is when a substance changes from liquid to gas.

6. In a physics change, matter changes in size, shape, or state without also changing identity.

7. One liquid is spread through another in an emotion.

8. Stored energy is pretentious energy.

9. The giving off of infrared rays through space is radical.

Word Wheel

Start with the letter A. Write it on the first line below the puzzle. Now write down every third letter. (The next letter has a star next to it to help you.)

Continue around the wheel, writing down every third letter. After you go around three times, you'll have an important message.

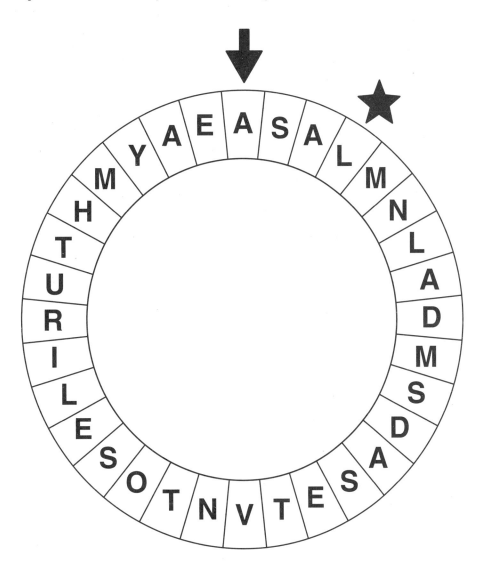

©Macmillan/McGraw-Hill

___ ___ ___ ___ ___ ___ ___ ___ ___ ___ ___ ___ ___

___ ___ ___ ___, ___ ___ ___ ___ ___ ___,

___ ___ ___ ___ ___ ___ ___!

Newton's Laws of Motion

Make an idea web like the one shown below on a separate piece of paper. List facts from your book in each of the outer web circles. Then write your conclusion in the center square. You can see if your conclusion is correct checking it against each of the facts that you listed. Each fact should support your conclusion. Look at the example below.

"Objects accelerate steadily as they fall."

"When the effects of air resistance are removed, objects of different weights fall at the same rate."

"An object's weight (or mass) does not affect how fast it accelerates when falling."

"Therefore, objects with greater mass fall with the same acceleration as less massive objects."

"Objects with a large mass are pulled by gravity with more force, but they also have more inertia."

"Objects are pulled to Earth by gravity."

© Macmillan/McGraw-Hill

Draw Conclusions

Conclusions should be based on facts and evidence, not on guesswork. It can help to number the known facts and separately list them. After proposing your conclusion, work backwards and see if each of the facts supports your conclusion. **Look at the paragraph below about acceleration. List the facts that lead to the conclusion below.**

What if you use a rubber band to launch a toy car along the floor? The rubber band will apply a force to the car, and the force will cause the car to speed up. Once the rear of the car passes the starting line, however, the rubber band no longer is applying force. At this point the car will begin coasting until friction brings it to a stop. The farther the car travels before stopping, the faster it must have been going at the start. When you add extra rubber bands you are applying more force to the car. As the force increases, the distance the car travels also increases.

Conclusion: The car reaches its greatest starting speed when the force applied to it is greatest.

More Drawing Conclusions

Conclusions are based on facts and evidence. Read the paragraph below.

After reviewing the facts in the paragraph, underline the correct conclusion from the following list.

There is a story that says that a falling apple may have set Isaac Newton to thinking about gravity. In the late 1660's there was a plague (very bad illness that spread very easily) in Cambridge, England where Newton had gone to college. To avoid the plague, he went home to the countryside. The legend says Newton was sitting under an apple tree one day, when an apple hit him on the head. The legend may or may not be true. However, an idea did hit Newton. That idea was that the force that pulls an apple to the ground is the same force that keeps the moon in its orbit around Earth.

Conclusion

1. Isaac Newton got the plague and that caused him to discover gravity.

2. The apple falling on Newton's head told him about the concept of gravity.

3. The legend about an apple falling on Newton's head is not true but he did come up with an idea about forces.

4. Newton came up with the idea that the force that pulls an apple to the ground is the same force that keeps the moon in its orbit around Earth.

© Macmillan/McGraw-Hill

Newton's First Law

Fill in the blanks. Reading Skill: **Draw Conclusions** - questions 6, 9, 15

What Does It Take to Make an Object Move?

1. A pull or push that acts on an object is called a _____.

2. Forces are needed to set objects in _____.

3. The _____ of an object tends to make the object resist being set into motion.

4. The tendency of an object to resist a change in its state of motion is called the object's _____.

5. Galileo imagined rolling a ball down a fixed _____ and then back up ramps of varying steepness.

6. Without a force to stop or slow a coasting object, the object will coast forever in a _____ line.

Is Force Needed to Maintain Motion?

7. _____ opposes the motion of one object moving past another.

8. _____ published a complete description of the concept of inertia.

9. Objects at rest remain at rest and objects traveling at a steady rate in a straight line continue that way until a _____ acts on them.

10. _____ first law of motion tells us that if an object is sitting at rest, it will continue to be at rest until a force is applied to it.

Where Is It?

11. You are moving when you are changing _____.

12. Position is the _____ of an object.

13. The _____ of a moving object is how fast its position is changing with time at any moment.

What Is Velocity?

14. The speed of a moving object taken together with its direction of travel gives the _____ of the object.

15. Two objects can have the same speed but different velocities if they are traveling in different _____.

What Is Acceleration?

16. As long as an object travels in a straight line at a steady speed, its velocity is _____.

17. A change in velocity is called _____.

18. _____ occurs when a force causes the speed of an object to decrease.

What Keeps Things Moving In a Circle?

19. _____ is the force that keeps Earth moving in a circular path about the Sun.

What Does It Take to Make an Object Move?

Galileo reasoned, a ball rolling down one ramp and up another would roll to the same height on any ramp. He tested his hypothesis in an experiment to determine how inertia affects the motion of a ball rolling down a fixed ramp and then up ramps of varying steepness as shown in the picture below.

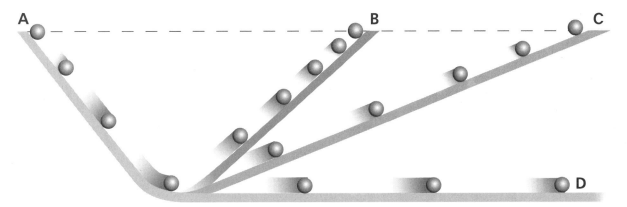

Answer the following questions about the picture above.

1. What might be acting on the ball to make it stop at points B and C?

   _____

2. Could you assemble a ramp that allowed a ball that started at point A to rise to a height that would be higher than the line drawn through points A and B?

   _____

   _____

3. If the ball traveled from point A up ramp B and stopped at point B, would it remain there indefinitely?

   _____

   _____

©Macmillan/McGraw-Hill

Where Is It?

The diagram below shows the shadow of an airliner moving over a town at a steady speed. One second passes between each position.

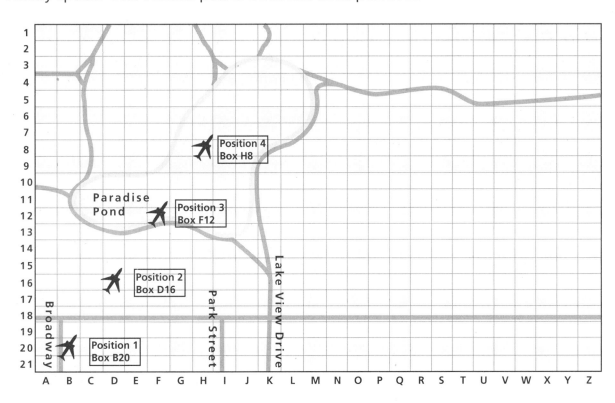

Answer the following questions about the picture above.

1. If the plane continues to travel in the same direction and reaches I7 on the grid one second after passing through H8, has its speed changed?

   _____

   _____

2. How would the speed of the plane have changed if the plane reaches I7 on the grid two seconds after passing through H8?

   _____

   _____

3. How would the speed of the plane have changed if the plane reaches L1 on the grid in less than a second after passing through H8?

   _____

   _____

Newton's First Law

Fill in the blanks.

Vocabulary

deceleration

velocity

acceleration

speed

inertia

friction

position

force

1. A force called _____ opposes the motion of one object moving past another.

2. _____ is the location of an object.

3. A pull or push that acts on an object is called a _____.

4. A change in velocity is called _____.

5. The _____ of an object is how fast its position is changing with time at any moment.

6. The tendency of an object to resist a change in its state of motion is called the object's _____.

7. _____ occurs when a force causes the speed of an object to decrease.

8. The speed of a moving object taken together with its direction of travel gives the _____ of an object.

Answer each question.

9. What are two ways that an object's velocity can change?

_____

_____

10. Describe two forces that can affect an object's velocity.

_____

_____

Newton's First Law

Vocabulary

inertia	deceleration	gravity	straight
velocity	law	direction	acceleration

Fill in the blanks.

As long as an object travels in a straight line at a steady speed, its

_____ is constant. Newton's first _____ tells

us that an object's velocity will remain constant unless a force is applied to it.

A force may change an object's speed, or its _____ of travel,

or both. A change in an object's velocity is called _____.

Newton realized that applying a force to an object would overcome its

_____ and change its velocity, causing it to accelerate.

A special case of acceleration, called _____, occurs

when a force causes the speed of an object to decrease. A force called

_____ pulls on Earth and keeps Earth moving in a circular

path about the Sun. Without the force of gravity, Earth would fly off in a

_____ line into deep space.

©Macmillan/McGraw-Hill

Lesson Outline
Lesson 2

Newton's Second and Third Laws

Fill in the blanks. Reading Skill: **Draw Conclusions** - question 7

What Affects Acceleration?

1. Sir Isaac Newton realized that forces produce _____.

2. If a force is applied to an object, the object's _____ will change.

3. If the _____ applied to an object is multiplied by a certain amount, the acceleration will change by the same amount.

4. Doubling the mass of an object results in _____ the acceleration.

5. Increasing the force increases the acceleration, while increasing the _____ decreases the acceleration.

6. When an object's mass is multiplied by a certain factor, the new acceleration is obtained by _____ the old acceleration by that factor.

7. The relationship between acceleration and mass is _____ —when one goes up, the other goes down.

How Is Acceleration Calculated?

8. A force of 1 _____ makes the speed of a 1-kg mass change by 1 meter per second each second.

9. We can write a(n) _____ to show how change in speed is related to force and mass.

Fill in the blanks.

What Are Balanced and Unbalanced Forces?

10. When all of the forces on an object cancel one another out, the forces are said to be _____ forces.

11. In cases where a certain force is either only partially canceled or not canceled at all by other forces, the force is said to be an _____ force.

Where Does the Force Come From?

12. If an object is accelerating it must have an _____ force acting on it.

How Do Forces Act Between Objects?

13. When one object applies a force to a second object, that force is called the _____.

14. The force that a second object returns to the first object is called the _____.

15. Newton realized that while the action and reaction act in opposite directions, they have the same _____.

16. Newton's _____ law of motion states that for every action, there is an equal but opposite reaction.

17. If the action and reaction forces between two objects are not balanced by other forces, _____ objects will accelerate.

How Can You Tell When Forces Are Acting?

18. Unbalanced forces reveal their action by causing _____.

© Macmillan/McGraw-Hill

Where Does the Force Come From?

The pictures below show the forces at work in a closed and an open balloon. The balloon can be used to illustrate Newton's second and third laws about balanced and unbalanced forces.

⬅ **Push of stretched rubber on air**
⬅ **Return push of air on rubber**

Answer the following questions about the picture above.

1. How are the forces inside of the closed balloon balanced?

_____

_____

2. Forces A and B are examples of what kinds of balanced forces?

_____

_____

3. Opening the balloon creates an unbalanced force that results in what kind of reaction force?

_____

_____

How Can You Tell When Forces Are Acting?

The picture below shows two different situations. In the first instance, the spring scale is pulling the cart at a constant speed. In the second instance, the spring scale is pulling the cart with extra force which accelerates the cart.

Answer the following questions about the picture above.

1. How does the graph in the first picture illustrate the cart's constant speed?

    _____

    _____

2. If the pull applied to the spring scale in the first picture stopped, what force would stop the cart from continuing to move at a constant speed?

    _____

    _____

3. Compare the cup of water and flag in each of the pictures. Why do you think that the water in the cup and the flag are affected in the second picture and not in the first picture?

    _____

    _____

©Macmillan/McGraw-Hill

Newton's Second and Third Laws

Fill in the blanks.

Vocabulary

velocity

balanced forces

multiplied

newtons

reaction

unbalanced force

action

1. When the mass of an object is _____ by a certain factor, the object's new acceleration is obtained by dividing the old acceleration by that factor.

2. Forces are often measured in _____.

3. In cases where a certain force is either partially canceled out or not cancelled out at all by other forces, the force is said to be a(n) _____.

4. Sir Isaac Newton realized that if a force is applied to an object, the object's _____ will change.

5. The force that a second object returns to the first object is called the _____.

6. When all of the forces on an object cancel one another out, the forces are said to be _____.

7. When one object applies a force to a second, we call this force the _____.

Answer each question.

8. Explain how you might experience a change of acceleration in a car.

_____

_____

_____

9. What is Newton's third law of motion?

_____

_____

Newton's Second and Third Laws

Vocabulary

equal	reaction	action	third
force	strength	balanced forces	unbalanced force

Fill in the blanks.

A pull or push that acts on an object is called a(n) _____.

When all of the forces on an object cancel one another out, the forces are

said to be _____. In cases where a certain force is either only

partially cancelled or not cancelled at all by other forces, the force is said to

be a(n) _____.

When one object applies a force to a second, we call this force the

_____. The force the second object returns to the first is

called the _____. Sir Isaac Newton realized that while the

action and reaction act in opposite directions, they have the same

_____. These ideas are summarized in Newton's

_____ law of motion: For every action, there is an

_____ but opposite reaction.

Newton's Law of Gravitation

Fill in the blanks. 📖 Reading Skill: **Draw Conclusions** - questions 1, 2

Why Would Air Make a Difference?

1. Air offers _____ to the motion of objects through it.

What Makes Objects Fall at the Same Rate?

2. Galileo concluded that objects accelerate steadily as they fall and that an object's weight, or _____ does not affect how fast it accelerates when falling.

3. An object is pulled to Earth by _____, an attraction between the mass of Earth and the mass of an object.

4. Objects with a large mass are pulled on by gravity with more force, but they also have more _____.

What Is the Acceleration of Falling Objects?

5. The force of gravity on any object is called its _____.

6. An object's weight in newtons can be found by multiplying its mass in kg by _____.

7. The _____ of any object falling to the ground increases by 9.8 meters per second each second.

8. A combination of the Moon's inertia and the force of gravity between Earth and the Moon keeps the Moon _____ Earth.

How Can Gravity Be Universal?

9. Newton decided that as mass _____, the force of gravity also increases.

10. Newton's law of universal _____ states that the force of gravity between two objects increases with the mass of the objects and decreases with the distance between them squared.

11. For light objects the force of gravity is _____.

12. For _____ objects like moons, planets, and stars, the masses are so large that the force of gravity becomes very large.

When Is Added Weight Helpful?

13. We are accustomed to gravity giving things on Earth weight, including our own _____.

14. In cycling, the weight of the rider and bicycle presses the tires against the ground causing friction, which gives the tires _____ and drives the rider forward.

What Makes Objects Fall at the Same Rate?

The picture below shows how gravity affects objects of different masses. According to Newton's second law, force equals mass multiplied by acceleration or F = ma. The acceleration of gravity changes slightly depending on how far away you are from Earth's center. However, since it varies only slightly, the acceleration of Earth's gravity can be rounded to equal 9.8 meters per second each second. Use this number to represent the acceleration in each of the following questions.

Answer the following questions about the picture above.

1. If the 1 kg object is being pulled by gravity by a force of 9.8 newtons, how many newtons of force does gravity exert on the 2 kg object?

   _____

   _____

2. If acceleration equals force divided by mass, what is the acceleration of each object if the force of gravity on the 1 kg object is 9.8 newtons and the force of gravity on the 2 kg object is 19.6 newtons? Note: acceleration is expressed as meters per second each second.

   _____

3. How many newtons of force would gravity exert on a 3 kg object?

   _____

What Is the Acceleration of Falling Objects?

The picture below shows the moon's orbit around Earth. The force of Earth's gravity keeps the moon accelerating towards Earth. Otherwise, the moon would fly off into space.

If there were no force pulling the Moon inward, it would fly off into space along this line.

To stay on the orbital path, the Moon must accelerate in this direction. The force pulling it inward causes the acceleration. Therefore, the Moon is accelerating toward Earth. The acceleration is caused by gravity.

The Moon's speed in its orbit is 1,030 m/scd

Answer the following questions about the picture above.

1. The moon moves at a constant speed of what around its orbit?

   _____

   _____

2. Is the moon's acceleration expressed as a change in speed or a change in direction?

   _____

   _____

3. If the moon was suddenly released from Earth's gravity what would happen to it? Would it still be experiencing acceleration?

   _____

   _____

Newton's Law of Gravitation

Fill in the blanks.

Vocabulary

gravity

inertia

resistance

universal

weight

distance

9.8

1. The force of gravity on any object is called the object's _____.

2. The force of gravity between two objects increases with the mass of the objects and decreases with the _____ between them squared.

3. If we ignore air resistance, all objects accelerate to the ground at _____ meters per second each second.

4. Scientists have learned that when the effects of air _____ are removed, objects of different weights fall at the same rate.

5. Newton's law of gravity is _____ because it applies to any objects, not just moons, planets, and stars.

6. An object is pulled to Earth by _____, an attraction between the mass of Earth and the mass of the object.

7. A combination of the Moon's _____ and the force of gravity between Earth and Moon keeps the Moon orbiting Earth.

Answer each question.

8. Explain how added weight might help to keep a car on the road from spinning off a sharp turn. _____

_____

_____

9. How did Galileo test his theories about objects of different masses falling at the same rate? _____

_____

_____

Newton's Law of Gravitation

Vocabulary

weights	ramps	accelerate
Galileo	resistance	mass
gravity	Aristotle	inertia

Fill in the blanks.

_____ believed that heavy things fall faster than lighter

things. Later, _____ reasoned that objects fall at the same

rate, ignoring air resistance. To test his ideas about falling objects,

Galileo carried out experiments that involved rolling marbles down

_____. He also talked about dropping two objects with dif-

ferent _____ off a tall tower to show that they would hit the

ground at the same time. Galileo concluded that objects _____

steadily as they fall and that an object's weight or _____ does

not affect how fast it accelerates when falling.

We know today that Galileo was right. An object is pulled to Earth by

_____, an attraction between the mass of the Earth and the

mass of the object. Objects with a large mass are pulled on by gravity with

more force, but they also have more _____. This extra

_____ to motion exactly offsets the greater pull of gravity on

them. Therefore, objects with greater mass fall with the same acceleration as

less massive objects.

© Macmillan/McGraw-Hill

● # Newton's Laws of Motion

Circle the letter of the best answer.

1. A force that opposes the motion of one object moving past another is
   a. gravity.
   b. friction.
   c. acceleration.
   d. unbalanced.

2. A pull or push that acts on an object is called a(n)
   a. acceleration.
   b. speed.
   c. force.
   d. inertia.

3. A change in velocity is called
   a. force.
   b. gravity.
   c. friction.
   d. acceleration.

4. How fast an object is changing its position with time at any moment is its
   a. speed.
   b. velocity.
   c. force.
   d. acceleration.

5. The tendency of an object to resist a change in its state of motion is called the object's
   a. speed.
   b. inertia.
   c. velocity.
   d. friction.

6. Velocity is
   a. how fast an object is changing its position with time at any moment.
   b. the acceleration of an object towards Earth.
   c. the rate at which friction slows the speed of an object.
   d. the speed of a moving object taken together with its direction of travel.

7. An attraction between the mass of Earth and the mass of the object is called
   a. mass.
   b. speed.
   c. gravity.
   d. velocity.

©Macmillan/McGraw-Hill

Circle the letter of the best answer.

8. An unbalanced force is
   a. a force that pushes in a particular direction.
   b. the rate of acceleration multiplied by the mass of an object.
   c. a force either partially canceled out or not cancelled out at all by other forces.
   d. when all forces in a system equally push on each other.

9. The force of gravity between two objects increases as their masses
   a. increase.
   b. decrease.
   c. decelerate.
   d. accelerate.

10. The force that a second object returns to the first object is called the
    a. inertia.
    b. action.
    c. unbalanced force.
    d. reaction.

11. When the forces on an object cancel each other out, the forces are said to be
    a. unbalanced.
    b. balanced.
    c. a reaction.
    d. massive.

12. The force of gravity on any object is called the object's
    a. inertia.
    b. velocity.
    c. reaction force.
    d. weight.

13. The force that prevents different objects from falling at the same rate is called
    a. inertia.
    b. gravity.
    c. air resistance.
    d. acceleration.

14. The force by which an object is pulled to Earth by an attraction between the mass of Earth and the mass of the object is called
    a. gravity.
    b. friction.
    c. weight.
    d. acceleration.

© Macmillan/McGraw-Hill

Chapter Summary

1. What is the name of the chapter you just finished reading?

   _____

   _____

2. What are four vocabulary words you learned in the chapter?
   Write a definition for each.

   _____

   _____

   _____

   _____

   _____

   _____

   _____

   _____

3. What are two main ideas that you learned in this chapter?

   _____

   _____

   _____

   _____

   _____

   _____

© Macmillan/McGraw-Hill

Sound Energy

You can use a cause-and-effect diagram to show how one event causes a second event. Sometimes the second event can cause a third event, the third event can cause a fourth event, and so on. Complete the cause-and-effect diagram for **Sound Waves** shown below. The first step has already been filled in for you. Notice that the effect of the first step is also the cause of the second step. In the same way, the cause of the third step will be the same as the effect of the second step, and so on.

Sound Waves

	Cause	Effect
Step 1	A violin string vibrates.	Molecules of gases in the air next to the vibrating string vibrate.
Step 2		The vibration continues to spread.
Step 3	The vibrations spreading away from the vibrating string are sound waves.	
Step 4	The sound waves make parts inside your ear start to vibrate.	

Name_____ Date_____

Cause and Effect

Things don't just happen. Living things and forces make them happen. Whatever or whoever makes something happen is the **cause**; what happens is the **effect**.

Here's an example. The frequency of a very high note sung by a singer can actually shatter glass. Vibrating sound waves are the cause, and a broken glass is the effect.

As you read books, look for clues to what makes things happen. Watch for clue words like because and so that point out a cause and its effect. For example: *I missed the bus **because** I overslept* or *I overslept, **so** I missed the bus.*

Read each statement below. Then circle the cause and underline the effect.

1. My baby brother cried because he fell down.

2. The glass shattered when the singer hit a high note.

3. Because of the snowstorm, we had to cancel the game.

4. I had no clean shirts, so I washed the dirty ones!

5. Because I was sick last week, I missed the big math test.

6. I broke my glasses, so I can't see the assignment written on the board!

7. He can't cross the street when the DON'T WALK sign is on.

8. I have a lot of allergies, so I can't have a kitten.

9. I tripped over the toys you left on the floor!

10. I don't have any money, so I can't buy that CD.

Now make up two cause-and-effect statements. Ask a classmate to identify each cause and effect.

_____

_____

_____

© Macmillan/McGraw-Hill

If . . . then

Some special cause-and-effect statements are called **If . . . then** statements. They state that if one thing happens, then another thing will happen.

Most **If . . . then** statements are true. However, **If** the first thing isn't true, **then** the second thing could never happen. Here's an example: *If this month is April, then next month will be May.* If it is really April, then the second part is true. However, if today is December 3, tomorrow can't possibly be a day in May!

Read the If . . . then statements below. If the first thing can make the second thing happen, write *T* for *true*. If it can't, write *NT* for *not true*.

_____ 1. If Marcy takes ballet lessons, then she must be a very good dancer.

_____ 2. If I do well on the test, then I'll get a good grade.

_____ 3. If my brother is 15 years old, then next year he'll be 16.

_____ 4. If it's very hot today, then it'll be cool tomorrow.

_____ 5. If a wheel is round, then it must be a circle.

_____ 6. If I have a library card, then I can sign out books and take them home.

_____ 7. If blue is my favorite color, then it must be your favorite color, too.

_____ 8. If I'm asleep in bed, then I must be sick.

_____ 9. If you get your hair cut, then your hair will be shorter.

_____ 10. If sound waves travel, then they have to bounce off objects in their paths.

Now write two of your own If . . . then statements. Read them to your classmates. Let them decide if it's T or NT.

_____

_____

_____

_____

©Macmillan/McGraw-Hill

Sound Waves

Fill in the blanks. Reading Skill: **Cause and Effect** - questions 1, 5, 9, 11

What Makes Sound?

1. Sounds can be produced by a back and forth motion called a(n) _____.

2. Many vibrations that make sound are too _____ to see.

3. When you pluck a guitar string, you provide the _____ necessary for this vibration.

4. The instruments in each section of the orchestra have their own characteristic ways of producing sounds, because in each section different _____ vibrate.

5. What vibrates to produce sounds in the following instruments?

    a. drums, cymbals _____

    b. trumpet, tuba _____

    c. saxophone, clarinet _____

6. Sound is a vibration that travels through _____.

7. Matter can be in the form of a(n) _____, a(n) _____, or a(n) _____.

8. Some types of matter are made of pieces too small to be seen; these are called _____.

9. A vibrating string causes molecules of gas in the _____ next to it to vibrate, too.

10. A vibration that spreads away from a vibrating object is called a(n) _____.

Fill in the blanks.

What Else Can Sound Go Through?

11. Inside the ear, sound waves cause the parts inside to _____.

12. Sound waves can travel through _____, such as air, and also through _____ and _____.

What Makes Sound?

The chart below shows how various musical instruments create sound waves. Each instrument can produce sound in different ways. The chart shows which part of the instrument vibrates. Each category of instruments has a different part that vibrates.

How Sound Is Produced

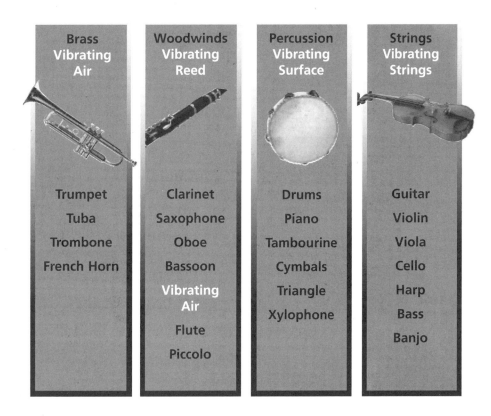

Brass Vibrating Air	Woodwinds Vibrating Reed	Percussion Vibrating Surface	Strings Vibrating Strings
Trumpet	Clarinet	Drums	Guitar
Tuba	Saxophone	Piano	Violin
Trombone	Oboe	Tambourine	Viola
French Horn	Bassoon	Cymbals	Cello
	Vibrating Air	Triangle	Harp
	Flute	Xylophone	Bass
	Piccolo		Banjo

Answer the following questions about the picture above.

1. What part of an oboe vibrates to cause the sound?

   _____

2. What part of the triangle vibrates to cause the sound?

   _____

3. What part of the guitar vibrates to cause the sound?

   _____

4. How are the trumpet and the flute similar?

   _____

Sound Waves

The picture below shows how the sound waves of a vibrating violin string travel. When the string vibrates, the molecules in the air first crowd together, and then they spread apart as the sound waves travel away from it.

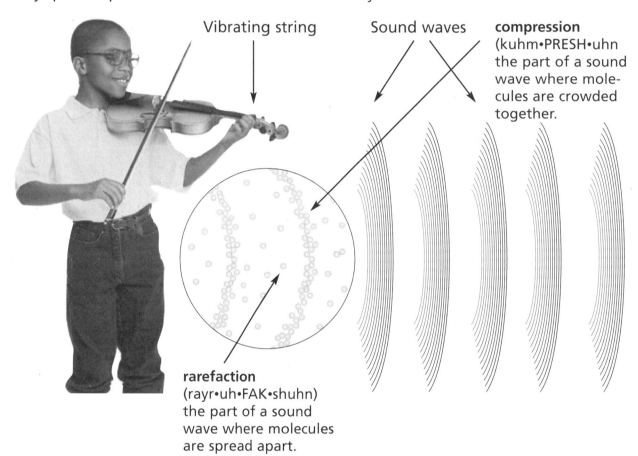

Vibrating string

Sound waves

compression (kuhm•PRESH•uhn the part of a sound wave where molecules are crowded together.

rarefaction (rayr•uh•FAK•shuhn) the part of a sound wave where molecules are spread apart.

Answer the following questions about the picture above.

1. Which part of the sound wave has molecules that are tightly packed together?

   _____

   _____

2. Which part of the sound wave has molecules that are spread apart?

   _____

3. What did the student do to produce the sound wave?

   _____

   _____

© Macmillan/McGraw-Hill

Sound Waves

Fill in the blanks.

1. A rapid back-and-forth movement is called a(n) _____.

2. Anything that has mass and takes up space is _____.

3. A percussion instrument makes sound with a vibrating _____.

4. The part of a sound wave where the molecules are crowded together is called _____.

5. Sound waves are collected in the human _____.

6. A vibration that spreads away from a vibrating object is a(n) _____.

7. The part of a sound wave where the molecules are spread apart is called _____.

Vocabulary

surface

ear

matter

vibration

rarefaction

sound wave

compression

Answer each question.

8. What sounds do you recognize as warnings or alerts?

_____

_____

9. Explain how sound made by a vibrating object travels.

_____

_____

_____

_____

_____

_____

© Macmillan/McGraw-Hill

Sound Waves

Vocabulary

sound wave	smallest	matter	molecules
gases	vibrate	ear	directions

Fill in the blanks.

Sound is a vibration that travels through _____. Some types

of matter are made of pieces too small to be seen, called _____.

Molecules are the _____ pieces that matter can be broken

into without changing the kind of matter. When a string vibrates, it makes

molecules of gases in the air next to it _____. A vibration that

spreads away from a vibrating object is a _____. It carries the

energy from the vibrating object outward in all _____. When

sound waves reach your _____, they make the parts inside

vibrate. Since air is a mixture of _____, you may conclude

that sound can travel through gases.

Pitch and Loudness

Fill in the blanks. Reading Skill: **Cause and Effect** - questions 2, 3, 7, 11, 13

What Is Pitch?

1. The term _____ refers to how high or low a sound is.

2. A shorter string vibrates faster and produces a(n) _____ than a longer string.

3. The pitch of a vibrating string is related to its _____ as well as its length.

4. The pitch of a person's voice varies with the length and thickness of the _____.

5. Scientists use a(n) _____ to picture sound waves and compare them.

6. The number of times an object vibrates per second is its _____.

7. A lower frequency produces a(n) _____ pitch; a higher frequency produces a(n) _____ pitch.

8. The unit for measuring frequency is the _____, which is abbreviated _____.

What Is Volume?

9. The back-and-forth distance that air molecules vibrate is based on how much _____ the sound wave carries.

10. A(n) _____ sound has more energy than a(n) _____ sound.

11. On an oscilloscope, a loud sound produces a(n) _____ wave than a soft sound does.

12. The unit for measuring volume is the _____.

Fill in the blanks.

How Is Sound Recorded?

13. In the first step of recording, sound waves cause vibrations in the
    _____ of a(n) _____, producing an
    electric current.

14. In the second step, a(n) _____ makes the current stronger.

15. Finally, the electric current arranges _____
    into patterns on a blank tape.

16. On a(n) _____, sound is stored by a computer code, not in
    magnetic patterns.

What Is Volume?

The pictures below show the differences in how a sound wave would look on an oscilloscope if the sound was low pitched, high pitched, loud, or soft. The length between each wavelength corresponds to the pitch of a sound and the height of each wavelength corresponds to the volume of a sound.

1

2

3

4

Answer the following questions about the picture above.

1. Which of the oscilloscope pictures shows the highest pitched sound?

_____

2. What is the main difference between the sounds shown in pictures 1 and 2, pitch or volume?

_____

_____

3. The distance between the arrows in pictures 1 and 2 corresponds to what?

_____

_____

4. The distance between the arrows in pictures 3 and 4 corresponds to what?

_____

_____

©Macmillan/McGraw-Hill

How Is Sound Recorded?

This diagram illustrates the inside of a microphone, showing how sound waves produce an electric current that transmits sound. To understand a diagram like this, read the labels and follow the leader lines to identify each part of the object. Then read the description of what happens in a microphone. Relate each step to the diagram.

Sound waves make the diaphragm in the microphone vibrate. That makes the coil of wire vibrate, sending an electric pattern to an amplifier.

Electric current

Sound waves

Diaphragm

Magnet

Wire coil

Microphone

Answer these questions about the diagram above.

1. A microphone changes sound waves into a(n) _____.

2. What do sound waves strike when they reach the head of the microphone? _____

3. The vibrations of the diaphragm cause vibrations in the _____.

4. An electric current is produced by the vibrating coil and the nearby _____.

5. The electric pattern is sent to a(n) _____.

©Macmillan/McGraw-Hill

Pitch and Loudness

Fill in the blanks.

1. High and low are words that describe the
   _____ of a sound.

2. The more energy a sound wave carries, the greater the
   _____.

3. A thicker guitar string produces a(n) _____
   sound than a thinner string because it vibrates
   more slowly.

4. An instrument that "pictures" sound waves is a(n)
   _____.

5. Higher pitched sound waves have a greater
   _____.

6. Frequency is measured in units called _____.

7. A sound's loudness is measured in _____.

8. Blank recording tapes are coated with scrambled _____.

Answer each question.

9. How is a drum different from a guitar? Compare the way they make sounds.

   _____

   _____

   _____

10. Would you keep a magnet in the same drawer as you keep your tapes? Why or
    why not?

    _____

    _____

Pitch and Loudness

Vocabulary

hertz	decibels	pitch	frequency
vibrations	related	oscilloscope	

Fill in the blanks.

You can't see sound waves, but scientists study them with a(n)

_____. This device makes a "picture" of sound waves.

_____ is the number of times an object vibrates per second.

Frequency describes _____ and sound waves.

_____ describes how your brain interprets a sound. Frequency

and pitch are _____: the higher the frequency, the higher the

pitch; the lower the frequency the lower the pitch. Frequency is measured in

units called _____. Volume, or how loud or soft a sound is, is

measured in units called _____.

©Macmillan/McGraw-Hill

Reflection and Absorption

Fill in the blanks. Reading Skill: **Cause and Effect** - questions 3, 5, 10, 15, 16, 17, 20

Do Sounds Bounce?

1. When a sound wave hits a surface, some of its energy bounces, or _____, off the surface.

2. Some energy from the sound wave goes into the surface in the process called _____.

3. How much of the sound is reflected or absorbed depends on the kind of material of the _____.

4. A(n) _____ surface absorbs more sound than a hard surface.

5. In a concert hall, too much _____ causes a hollow, empty sound.

6. When a music hall was built in the 1870s, people's clothing _____ more sound than did styles in the 1930s.

What Is an Echo?

7. A reflected sound wave is called a(n) _____.

How Fast Is Sound?

8. In air at room temperature, sound waves travel at a speed of _____ per second.

9. Sound waves generally travel faster in _____ than in _____ and _____.

10. The speed of sound waves depends largely on the _____ of the material.

11. Temperature affects the speed of sound more in _____ than in liquids and solids.

What Can Echoes Do?

12. Sonar uses _____ to detect faraway objects.

13. To measure ocean depths, a sonar technician times how long sound waves take to bounce off distant objects and _____.

14. Animals like whales and bats use a form of sonar called _____ to find their way or locate food.

How Do Moving Sounds Change?

15. As a siren or train whistle moves toward you, the pitch of the sound gets _____.

16. When a sound source moves toward you, the _____ of the sound increases.

17. As the sound source moves away, the sound waves spread, decreasing the _____ and lowering the _____.

18. The change in frequency and pitch as a source of sound moves toward or away from you is known as the _____.

What Is Fundamental Frequency?

19. The lowest frequency of any sound is its _____.

20. The blend of the fundamental frequency and the _____ produced gives each sound its own _____.

21. Bridges have collapsed as a result of _____.

What Can Echoes Do?

This diagram shows two ways sound waves are used to locate objects and measure their distance. Human technicians use sonar technology to measure depths in different parts of the ocean. Whales use a form of sonar called echolocation. To understand the diagram, look carefully at the drawing and read the labels.

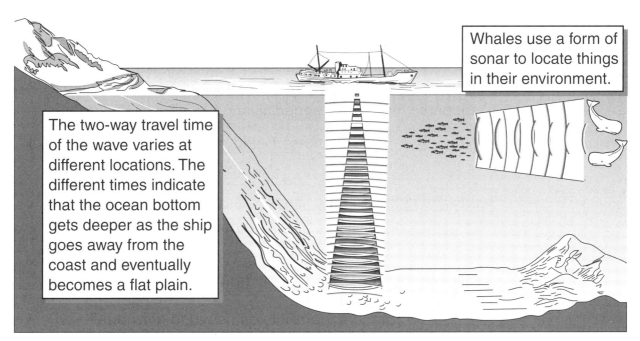

Whales use a form of sonar to locate things in their environment.

The two-way travel time of the wave varies at different locations. The different times indicate that the ocean bottom gets deeper as the ship goes away from the coast and eventually becomes a flat plain.

Answer these questions about the diagram above.

1. What is sonar used for on the ship?

_____

2. How can scientists on the ship tell that the depth of the ocean bottom changes as the ship moves away from the coast?

_____

3. What happens to the travel time of the wave when the ship is over the flat plain?

_____

4. How is the whale using its form of sonar?

_____

© Macmillan/McGraw-Hill

How Do Moving Sounds Change?

The pictures below show how the pitch of a sound wave changes as it approaches and moves away from a listener.

1

2

Sound waves from the moving police car bunch together (1) as the car approaches the listener. They spread apart (2) as the police car moves away from listener.

Answer the following questions about the picture above.

1. Would the sound waves of a blaring siren on a police car bunch together or spread apart as it approaches the listener?

_____

2. Would the pitch of the siren get higher or lower as the police car approaches the listener? Why?

_____

_____

3. Would the sound waves bunch together or spread apart as the police car moves away from the listener?

_____

4. Would the pitch of the siren get higher or lower as the police car moves away from the listener? Why?

_____

_____

© Macmillan/McGraw-Hill

Reflection and Absorption

Fill in the blanks.

1. The disappearance of a sound wave into a surface is called _____.

2. The bouncing of a sound wave off a surface is called _____.

3. The lowest frequency at which a string vibrates is called _____.

4. _____ is when strings are vibrating at higher frequencies at the same time as the fundamental frequency.

5. The build-up of vibrations at natural frequency is called _____.

6. Many animals use a form of sonar called _____.

7. A change in frequency and pitch as sound moves toward and away is called the _____.

8. A reflected sound wave is called a(n) _____.

9. _____ depends on the blend of fundamental frequencies and overtones.

Answer this question.

10. What is the Doppler effect?

_____

_____

_____

_____

Reflection and Absorption

Vocabulary

dolphin	prey	sound waves	sight
echo	echolocation	ears	

Fill in the blanks.

Sonar uses _____ to detect objects far away. A form of sonar called _____ helps animals locate things around them. Bats use this instead of _____ to navigate. They send out squeals toward their _____. Bats pick up the reflected sounds using their large _____. Another animal that uses sonar to locate objects is the _____. You also use reflected sound when you shout hello and make a(n) _____.

©Macmillan/McGraw-Hill

Sound Energy

Circle the letter of the best answer.

1. The disappearance of a sound wave into a surface is called
   a. reflection.   b. absorption.
   c. sonar.   d. energy.

2. The part of a sound wave where molecules are crowded together is called the
   a. rarefaction.   b. vibration.
   c. matter.   d. compression.

3. All sound waves are created by
   a. vibrations.   b. instruments.
   c. plucking a string.   d. striking a surface.

4. The part of a sound wave where molecules are spread apart is called the
   a. compression.   b. rarefaction.
   c. loudness.   d. tone.

5. Frequency is measured in units called
   a. waves.   b. hertz.
   c. radio waves.   d. decibels.

6. Volume is measured in units called
   a. frequency.   b. loudness.
   c. hertz.   d. decibels.

© Macmillan/McGraw-Hill

Circle the letter of the best answer.

7. A vibration that spreads away from a vibrating object is a
   a. hertz.
   b. compression.
   c. sound wave.
   d. frequency.

8. The bouncing of a sound wave off a surface is called
   a. reflection.
   b. absorption.
   c. compression.
   d. rarefaction

9. The blend of the fundamental frequencies and overtones gives each sound its own
   a. diaphragm.
   b. vibration.
   c. quality.
   d. magnet.

10. When a sound wave is absorbed, its sound energy is changed into
    a. electrical energy.
    b. light energy.
    c. mechanical energy.
    d. heat energy.

11. To hear an echo, you must have
    a. a mountain.
    b. a shower stall.
    c. a good reflective surface.
    d. a high-tech recording system.

12. When a string vibrates at the fundamental frequency, sections of the string vibrate at a higher frequency called a(n)
    a. reflection.
    b. overtone.
    c. diaphragm.
    d. hertz.

©Macmillan/McGraw-Hill

Chapter Summary

1. What is the name of the chapter you just finished reading?

   _____

   _____

2. What are four vocabulary words you learned in the chapter?
   Write a definition for each.

   _____

   _____

   _____

   _____

   _____

   _____

   _____

   _____

3. What are two main ideas that you learned in this chapter?

   _____

   _____

   _____

   _____

   _____

   _____

   _____

© Macmillan/McGraw-Hill

Light Energy

You can use a compare and contrast table to show how two or more items are alike and how they are different. Look at the example shown below for primary colors and primary pigments. The two shaded boxes list the two items being compared. The first column of the table lists the characteristics of the items being compared.

Characteristic	Primary Color	Primary Pigment
Number	3	3
Colors	red, green, blue	magenta, cyan, yellow
Color when mixed together equally	white	black
Refers to	colors of light	colors of pigments, such as paint

Make a compare and contrast table for concave mirrors and convex mirrors.

Characteristic	Concave Mirrors	Convex Mirrors
Curve of shiny surface		
Inside or outside of soup spoon		
More than one type of image?		
Type of image(s)		

Make a compare and contrast table for infrared light and ultraviolet light.

Characteristic	Infrared Light	Ultraviolet Light
Wavelength compared to visible light		
Source		
Effect		

© Macmillan/McGraw-Hill

Compare and Contrast

Remember that to compare things, you look for ways the things are alike. To contrast them, you look for ways they are different.

In the exercise below, finish each sentence. The word in parentheses ( ) tells you whether to compare or contrast the two things. The first one has been done for you.

1. (compare) My brother is <u>as tall as I am.</u>

2. (contrast) The boys in our class are _____.

3. (contrast) Isn't that car _____?

4. (compare) Your new house is _____.

5. (contrast) Her hair is _____.

6. (compare) Our math teacher is _____.

7. (contrast) I think this movie is _____.

8. (contrast) My mother's cooking is _____.

9. (compare) Yesterday's weather was _____.

10. (contrast) Your cousin _____.

11. (compare) That painting _____.

12. (compare) They said our songs _____.

13. (contrast) This candidate for mayor _____.

14. (contrast) Those jeans _____.

15. (compare) Your computer _____.

Something in Common

An **analogy** is a special way to compare things that are different by finding something they have in common. For example, a tadpole is a young frog, and a puppy is a young dog. We can say that *tadpole is to frog as puppy is to dog*. That's an analogy!

Read each example below. Think about the relationship between the first two words. **Then circle the correct word to complete each analogy.**

1. **Ears** are to **sound** as **eyes** are to _____.

   odors   light   tastes

2. **Rug** is to **floor** as **curtain** is to _____.

   chair   bed   window

3. **Elephants** are to **herd** as **geese** are to _____.

   school   flock   pride

4. **Wing** is to **plane** as **sail** is to _____.

   boat   car   train

5. **Evergreen** is to **tree** as **orchid** is to _____.

   weed   fruit   flower

6. **Foot** is to **sneaker** as **hand** is to _____.

   ring   glove   blanket

7. **Knife** is to **knives** as **life** is to _____.

   living   lived   lives

8. **Duet** is to **two** as **trio** is to _____.

   four   three   five

Light and Mirrors

Fill in the blanks. Reading Skill: **Compare and Contrast** - questions 5, 11, 14, 15

Can You See Without Light?

1. The Moon shines only because it reflects _____.

2. We cannot see the dark half of the Moon because

   _____.

3. Light is a means of transferring _____ between points.

4. All the objects we can see either give off their own light or

   _____ from another source.

5. All these objects produce their own light in different ways that involve heat:

   a. _____ heat the Sun

   b. _____ heat a burner flame

   c. _____ heats the wire of a light bulb

6. Molecules in a hot material move swiftly and collide, giving off some energy

   as _____.

7. Any light source converts energy of some kind into _____.

Fill in the blanks.

How Does Light Travel?

8. The shadows that light casts suggest that light usually travels in

   _____.

9. If light passes from one substance into another, it usually

   _____.

10. A beam of light that is not disturbed or bent moves in a straight line as a(n)

    _____.

How Does Light Bounce Off Objects?

11. Light rays that reflect off _____ scatter in many directions, while light rays that reflect off a flat, polished surface create a mirror image.

12. According to the _____, the angle between an incoming light ray and the surface is _____ the angle between the surface and a reflected light ray.

13. Light rays that bounce off a mirror or other shiny surface reflect a picture, or _____.

How Do Curved Mirrors Form Images?

14. A mirror that curves in on the shiny side is _____, while a mirror that curves out on the shiny side is _____.

15. The image in a flat mirror is _____ and reversed left to right. The image formed by a _____ mirror may be right-side up or upside-down. It may be large or small, depending on how far the object is from the mirror.

©Macmillan/McGraw-Hill

How Does Light Travel?

How does light travel? This drawing shows a light bulb casting the shadow of a microscope onto a wall. If you study the diagram and the paths of the light rays, you can discover for yourself the kind of path that light rays follow. The light rays are lettered so you can identify them.

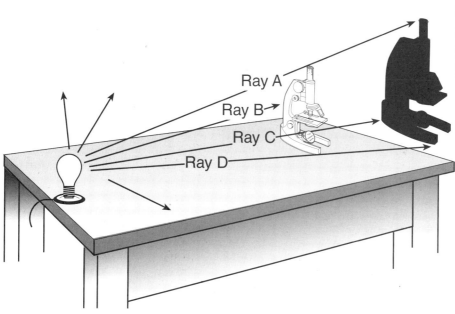

Ray A
Ray B
Ray C
Ray D

Light casting a shadow suggests that light travels in straight lines.

Answer these questions about the diagram above.

1. Which light ray passes above the top of the microscope and falls onto the wall? _____

2. A light ray is stopped by the microscope. Which is it? _____

3. Which light rays pass to the side of the microscope and light up the wall? _____

4. Explain in your own words why all the light rays don't go around the microscope and reach the wall.

_____

_____

5. What is the result of light rays being stopped by the microscope?

_____

How Do Curved Mirrors Form Images?

A concave mirror is one that curves inward on the shiny side. This diagram shows how such a curved mirror forms an image. To understand the diagram, notice the arrows that show the paths of two light rays as they reflect off the curved surface. Trace the path of each light ray as it travels toward the mirror and then is reflected back to the observer. Notice the positions of both the object and its mirror image.

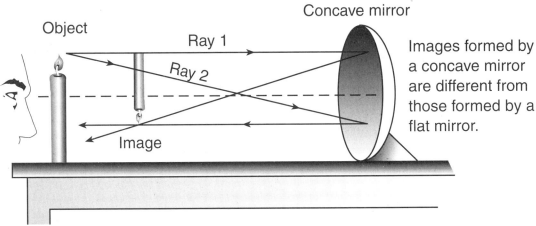

Images formed by a concave mirror are different from those formed by a flat mirror.

Answer these questions about the diagram above.

1. What does the dotted line in the diagram represent?

   _____

2. How does light ray 1 travel toward the mirror?

   _____

   How does it reflect off the curved surface? _____

3. How does light ray 2 travel toward the mirror?

   _____

   How does it reflect off the curved surface of the mirror?

   _____

4. How does the size of the image compare with the size of the original object?

   _____

5. In what other way is the mirror image different from the original object?

   _____

⚫ # Light and Mirrors

Fill in the blanks.

Vocabulary

concave

Law of reflection

energy

light ray

chemical

reflects

convex

1. We are able to see most things only because light
   _____ off them.

2. Light and sound are both means of transferring
   _____ between two points.

3. A straight beam of light is called a _____.

4. Some chemical reactions produce a(n)
   _____ form of light.

5. The _____ states the angle between an
   incoming light ray and a surface equals the angle
   between the reflected light ray and the surface.

6. A(n) _____ mirror is like the inside of a spoon.

7. A(n) _____ mirror always forms a reduced, upright image.

Answer each question.

8. You want to check out what is behind you using a mirror. How would knowing
   about the law of reflection help you position the mirror?

   _____

   _____

   _____

   _____

   _____

9. How does light behave like a wave?

   _____

   _____

   _____

   _____

Light and Mirrors

Vocabulary

concave	reversed	in	shiny
convex	rearview	image	

Fill in the blanks.

Light rays bouncing off a mirror reflect a picture called a(n)

_____. Although reflections in a flat mirror look real,

they are _____ from right to left. Telescopes often use

_____ mirrors. They curve _____ on the shiny

side. Mirrors that curve out on the _____ side are convex

mirrors. You've probably seen _____ mirrors used as a store's

security system. Convex mirrors are also used as side _____

mirrors in cars.

Light and Lenses

Fill in the blanks. Reading Skill: **Compare and Contrast** - questions 1, 7, 9, 12, 13, 17

What Can Light Pass Through?

1. Light easily passes through _____ materials but is completely blocked out by _____ materials.

2. Materials that let some light through, but give a blurry view, are called _____.

3. Light waves usually vibrate in all directions, but _____ allows only light vibrating in a certain direction to pass through.

4. In sunglasses, polarizing materials block _____ and other light that vibrates sideways.

5. Self-tinting glasses get darker or lighter because of a chemical containing silver particles that react to _____.

How Can Light Rays Be Bent?

6. The bending of light rays as they pass from one substance into another is called _____.

7. When light passes into a denser substance it _____.

8. A substance made of material that is more tightly packed together is _____ than one that is less tightly packed together.

9. If light enters a denser material directly, it continues in a straight path, but if it enters at an angle it is _____ into a new direction.

10. The amount of refraction _____ as the incoming angle gets shallower.

Fill in the blanks.

How Do Lenses Work?

11. A curved piece of transparent material that refracts light to make an image is a(n) _____.

12. The surfaces of a(n) _____ lens curve outward, while the surfaces of a(n) _____ lens curve inward.

13. A convex lens refracts light rays _____, while a concave lens refracts light rays _____.

How Does the Eye Work?

14. The lens in a human eye is a(n) _____ lens.

15. The lens in your eye casts an image onto a tissue called the _____, which converts it into nerve signals that go to the _____.

16. In the eye, light is refracted first by the _____ and then enters the eye through the pupil and travels to the _____.

17. In a(n) _____ eye, the lens focuses images short of the retina, while in a(n) _____ eye, the image is focused behind the retina.

© Macmillan/McGraw-Hill

How Does the Eye Work?

This diagram shows the different parts of the eye, which together allow you to see images. Follow the numbered labels to trace the path of light as it passes through the eye to form an image on the retina. Notice where the light rays are bent, or refracted, when they pass through different structures.

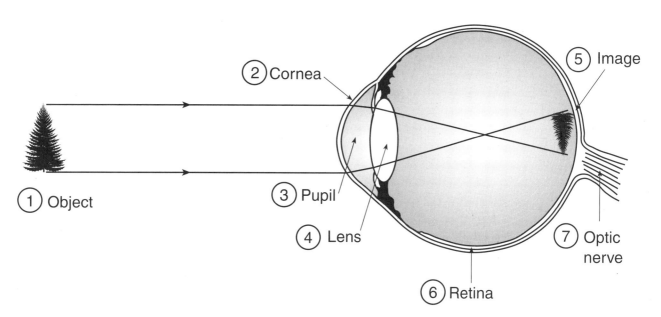

Answer these questions about the diagram above.

1. When light reaches the eye, it is refracted first as it passes through the _____.

2. The opening that lets light enter the eye is the _____.

3. Light then passes through the _____ and is bent still more, forming an image on the retina.

4. The nerve that carries images to the brain is called the _____.

How Glasses and Contact Lenses Work

These diagrams show how different kinds of lenses can correct certain kinds of vision problems. The lenses bend light rays so that the images fall on the retina. Carefully trace the paths of light rays in both types of eyes. Then notice how lenses bend the light differently.

Nearsighted Eye

Image Falls Short of Retina

Farsighted Eye

Image Falls Behind Retina

Lens allows image to fall on retina.

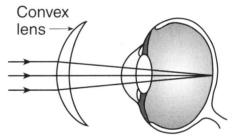

Lens allows image to fall on retina.

Answer these questions about the diagram above.

1. Which type of eye appears shorter from lens to retina?

_____

2. In a farsighted eye, does the image fall in front of the retina or behind the retina? _____

3. If a nearsighted person doesn't wear glasses or contact lenses, where does the image fall in the eye? _____

4. Look at the path of the light rays passing through the corrective lens for a nearsighted eye. Does the lens focus the light rays more sharply or spread them out? _____

5. A(n) _____ lens is used to correct nearsightedness.

© Macmillan/McGraw-Hill

Light and Lenses

Fill in the blanks.

Vocabulary

cornea

translucent

opaque

transparent

refraction

convex

polarization

concave

1. A(n) _____object will allow no light rays through.

2. The bending of light rays as they pass from one substance to another is called _____.

3. When only one direction of light vibrations can pass through a material it is called _____.

4. A lens that forms images by refracting light rays apart is a(n) _____ lens.

5. A lens that forms images by refracting light rays together is a(n) _____ lens.

6. Matter that is _____ will allow some light to pass through.

7. The _____ of your eye refracts the image it receives.

8. You can see clearly through any _____ object.

Answer each question.

9. How are self-tinting sunglasses different from polarized sunglasses? Which would you wear? Why?

_____

_____

_____

_____

10. Explain how lenses correct vision problems.

_____

_____

_____

_____

© Macmillan/McGraw-Hill

Light and Lenses

Vocabulary

direction	color	transparent	particles
polarization	waves	vibrate	materials

Fill in the blanks.

One interesting way for controlling light is called _____. Light

travels in _____. Normally these waves _____

in all different directions. Yet, light can be polarized by some

_____. Only one _____ of light vibration can

pass through these materials. Scientists have also used materials to develop

sunglasses that change _____. The lenses of self-tinting

glasses contain very small amounts of a _____, silver-contain-

ing chemical. When struck by bright light, this chemical turns into tiny silver

_____. These particles darken the glass in bright light.

Light and Color

Fill in the blanks. Reading Skill: **Compare and Contrast** - questions 3, 17

How Do You Get Color From White Light?

1. A(n) _____ is a triangular piece of polished glass that refracts white sunlight into a band of colors.

2. Newton called the band of colors a(n) _____.

3. A prism refracts _____ light the most, and _____ light the least.

4. If the spectrum made by a prism were passed through a second prism, the colors would recombine to produce _____.

5. A rainbow forms when raindrops act both as _____ and as _____ to reflect the colors to your eyes.

6. If the Sun is _____, you may see a rainbow in mist from a hose or fountain.

7. White light is a mixture of the entire _____ of colors.

How Do Colors Look in Colored Light?

8. A color filter _____ some colors of light and lets others pass through.

9. A red cellophane filter allows _____ to pass through but blocks _____.

10. If you look at a red tomato through a green filter, the tomato will appear _____.

11. The primary colors of light are _____, _____, and _____.

Fill in the blanks.

12. Cells in the _____ of the human eye react to colors of light.

13. If the retina is struck with equal amounts of red, green, and blue light, we see _____.

What Happens When Color Is Reflected?

14. A(n) _____ is a colored substance that reflects some colors and absorbs others.

15. The color of an object is due to the colors that it _____.

16. A green leaf _____ green light and _____ red and blue light.

17. A material that absorbs all colors appears _____, while one that reflects all colors appears _____.

18. When you mix colored lights, you _____ colors until you get white.

19. When you mix paints or pigments, you _____ colors until you get black.

20. The primary pigments are _____, _____, and _____.

How Do Colors Look in Colored Light?

The picture below shows how a red tomato would look if it were looked at through different colored filters. Red, green, and blue are considered to be the primary colors of light.

Red   Green   Blue

Panel 1   Panel 2   Panel 3

Answer the following questions about the picture above.

1. Why does the red tomato appear to be red under the red filter?

   _____

   _____

2. Why does the red tomato appear to be black under the green or blue filters?

   _____

   _____

   _____

3. What colors would a green apple appear to be under each of the filters?

   _____

   _____

©Macmillan/McGraw-Hill

What Happens When Color Is Reflected?

This diagram shows why different objects are different colors. Pigments in the object reflect or absorb certain colors of light. To understand the diagram, follow the path of the ray of light as it strikes a green leaf and then is reflected back to a person's eye. Notice what happens to the different colors in the light ray.

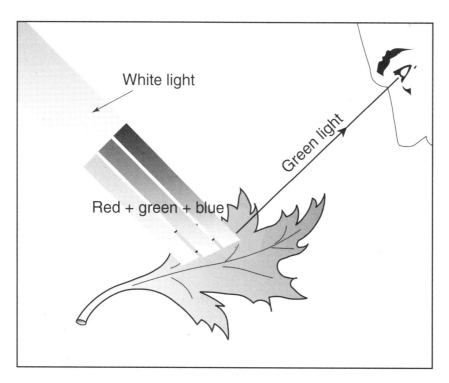

White light

Green light

Red + green + blue

Answer these questions about the diagram above.

1. What color is the ray of light that strikes the leaf? _____

2. A ray of white light is actually a blend of red, _____, and _____ light.

3. What color or colors of light does the green leaf absorb?

_____

4. What color or colors of light does the green leaf reflect? _____

5. Imagine that the light is striking a red rose instead of a green leaf. What color or colors would the rose absorb? _____

Light and Color

Fill in the blanks.

1. If you shine a light through a(n) _____, you can see a rainbow.

2. The _____ are red, green, and blue.

3. A prism will break light apart by color so you can see the whole _____.

4. An object that reflects all colors will appear _____.

5. The color violet is _____ more than any other color in the spectrum.

6. The _____ are magenta, cyan, and yellow.

7. An object that absorbs all colors will appear _____.

8. Cells in the eye's _____ allow us to see colors.

Answer each question.

9. How is mixing the colors of light different than mixing colors of paint?

_____

_____

_____

_____

10. What color filter or filters would make a red tomato appear red? Black?

_____

_____

_____

Vocabulary

spectrum

refracted

retina

black

prism

primary colors

white

primary pigments

© Macmillan/McGraw-Hill

Light and Color

Vocabulary				
refracts	magenta	rainbow	colors	sunlight
prism	primary	spectrum	drops	

Fill in the blanks.

Sir Isaac Newton discovered that when light goes through a(n)

_____ it produces a band of rainbow colors. He named this

color band a(n) _____. White sunlight is a mixture of many

_____. The prism _____ each color at a differ-

ent angle. Water _____ can also act like prisms. They can

break up rays of _____ into different colors. When this

occurs, a(n) _____ forms in the sky. We can paint these colors

ourselves by mixing _____ pigments. These include yellow,

_____, and cyan.

©Macmillan/McGraw-Hill

Invisible Light

Fill in the blanks. Reading Skill: **Compare and Contrast** - questions 7, 16

How Do Waves Move?

1. All waves carry _____ from place to place.

2. Without particles vibrating back and forth in the _____ that the sound is traveling, the energy of the sound vibration could not travel.

3. Sound waves cannot travel in a(n) _____, a space where there is no matter.

How Do Light Waves Travel?

4. Electricity and magnetism produce forces of _____.

5. Light is a form of _____.

6. The _____ of a wave is the distance from the crest of one wave to the crest of the next.

7. Electromagnetic waves vibrate back and _____ across the direction in which light travels.

8. The _____ of light are different wavelengths.

9. Different wavelengths of light travel through space at _____.

10. Another theory about how light travels suggests that it moves as bundles of energy called _____.

11. The human eye cannot see wavelengths of light that are _____ than red or _____ than violet.

12. Visible and invisible wavelengths of light together make up the _____.

Fill in the blanks.

Which Wavelengths Are Longer than Red Light?

13. The longest waves in the electromagnetic spectrum are _____.

14. A radar device uses _____ to locate objects.

Which Wavelengths Are Shorter than Violet Light?

15. Ultraviolet light can produce _____ in your body.

16. UV light from the Sun can cause a _____ as well as some forms of the disease _____.

17. Earth is protected from much of the Sun's UV light by the _____.

18. The shortest wavelengths in the spectrum are _____ and _____.

What Are Lasers?

19. Unlike light from most sources, a(n) _____ is a device that produces thin streams of light.

How Do Waves Move?

These drawings show how a moving wave affects a floating object. Compare the three drawings and notice how the crest of the wave moves forward.

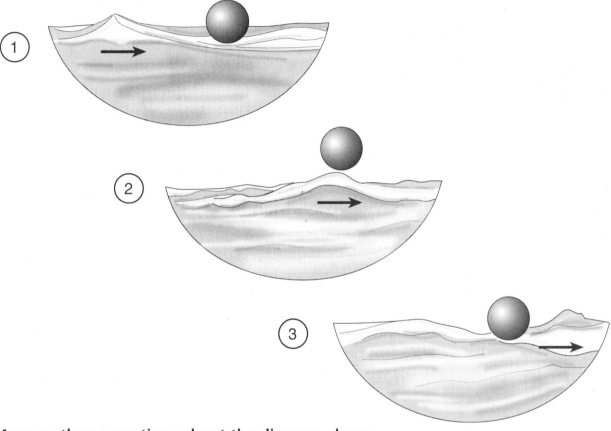

Answer these questions about the diagram above.

1. In which direction is the water wave moving?

_____

2. What happens to the ball when the wave crest reaches it?

_____

3. What happens to the ball after the wave crest passes it?

_____

4. Does the wave move the ball forward or backward? Explain your answer.

_____

_____

How Do Light Waves Travel?

This diagram shows the kinds of light—visible and invisible—that make up the electromagnetic spectrum. Read this diagram as you would a chart. Notice major categories and the smaller divisions within them. Look at the different ways in which the diagram presents information. It uses both measurements and drawings to show different wavelengths.

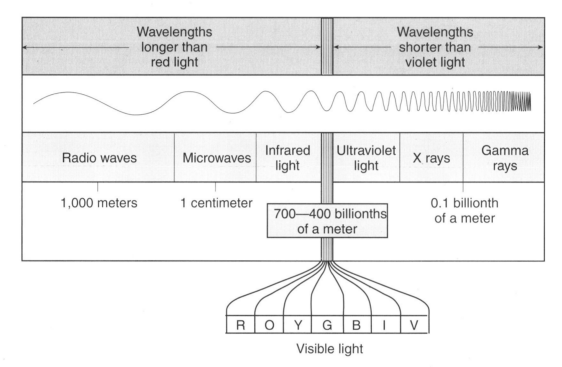

Visible light

Answer these questions about the diagram above.

1. Are infrared waves longer or shorter than red light?

   _____

2. Are ultraviolet rays longer or shorter than violet light?

   _____

3. The longest waves in the spectrum are _____.

4. Which rays have a longer wavelength—X rays or ultraviolet rays?

   _____

5. The wavelength of microwaves is _____.

6. In visible light, which color has the longest wavelength?

   _____

Invisible Light

Fill in the blanks.

1. Sound waves cannot travel in a _____.

2. Electromagnetic waves can travel with or without _____.

3. We cannot see _____ of light longer than the length of red light waves.

4. The longest waves of the electromagnetic specturm are _____ waves.

5. _____ refers to forces that come from electricity and magnetism.

6. Scientists believe that light may travel as tiny bundles of energy called _____.

7. _____ produce light that does not spread out or become weaker.

8. All of the wavelengths of light, the ones we see and the ones we cannot see, are called the _____.

Answer each question.

9. What instrument allows scientists to detect forms of light that they cannot see?

_____

_____

10. List, in order of longer to shorter wavelengths, the different waves of the electromagnetic specturm.

_____

_____

Invisible Light

Vocabulary

light	ranging	echo	signals
photons	electromagnetic spectrum	models	vibrating

Fill in the blanks.

Since James Clark Maxwell's work with electromagnetic energy, scientists have formed another idea of how light travels. Rather than as a smooth _____ wave, perhaps light travels as tiny bundles of energy. Scientists call the tiny bundles of energy _____. Waves or photons? Scientists use both _____ to explain light. Some invisible wavelengths of _____ are longer than red. Radar, short for radio detecting and _____, uses radio waves that reflect off objects. This is similar to how animals locate things using the _____ of sound waves. The longest waves of the _____ are radio waves. These waves carry _____ in AM or FM codes.

©Macmillan/McGraw-Hill

Light Energy

Circle the letter of the best answer.

1. A mirror that produces an upright, reduced image is a
   a. concave mirror.
   b. flat mirror.
   c. highly polished mirror.
   d. convex mirror.

2. A point on a light wave as it ripples outward from its source is a
   a. spectrum.
   b. light ray.
   c. spark.
   d. color pigment.

3. A lens that forms images by refracting light rays together is a
   a. convex lens.
   b. magnetic lens.
   c. concave lens.
   d. laser lens.

4. Concave mirrors
   a. form an image that is larger than the original object.
   b. form many different kinds of images.
   c. form an image that appears to be upside down.
   d. form an image that is smaller than the original object.

5. Materials with this property completely block light from passing through and are called
   a. concave.
   b. convex.
   c. transparent.
   d. opaque.

6. Clear glass is an example of a(n)
   a. transparent material.
   b. opaque material.
   c. mirror.
   d. translucent material.

©Macmillan/McGraw-Hill

7. When a material allows only part of the light to pass through it is called
   a. opaque.
   b. pigmented.
   c. translucent.
   d. transparent.

8. If an object appears to be red, it
   a. is red.
   b. reflects red light and absorbs all the other colors.
   c. absorbs red light and reflects all the other colors.
   d. has molecules of red which are more active than the other molecules.

9. A triangular piece of cut and polished glass is a
   a. mirror.
   b. lens.
   c. prism.
   d. laser.

10. Which is NOT a primary color of light?
    a. brown
    b. green
    c. blue
    d. red

11. What are the three primary pigments?
    a. yellow, red, and blue
    b. green, blue, and red
    c. magenta, cyan, and yellow
    d. magenta, cyan, and fuchsia

12. All the wavelengths of light, seen or unseen, are called the
    a. photons.
    b. prism.
    c. infrared waves.
    d. electromagnetic spectrum.

13. Laser beams are narrow and
    a. blue.
    b. red.
    c. direct.
    d. weak.

© Macmillan/McGraw-Hill

Meanings and Words

Vocabulary			
echo	inertia	frequency	vibration
transparent	concave	convex	opaque
refraction	weight	action	spectrum

Read each meaning. Then find a word in the Vocabulary Box that fits that meaning, and write it on the line.

Meanings	Words
1. a back-and-forth motion	_____
2. the number of times an object vibrates per second	_____
3. a reflected sound wave	_____
4. tendency of an object to resist a change in its state of motion	_____
5. completely blocking light passage	_____
6. the bending of light rays	_____
7. curves in	_____
8. curves out	_____
9. the force of gravity on any object	_____
10. a band of colors produced when light goes through a prism	_____
11. when one object applies a force to a second	_____
12. letting all light through	_____

©Macmillan/McGraw-Hill

Crossword

Read each clue. Write the answer.

Across

1. Unit that measures loudness
4. Unit for measuring frequency
6. Opposite of low
9. Back-and-forth motion
10. Tiny bundle of light energy
11. Bending light rays
13. How high or low a sound is
14. Difference between two sounds of the same pitch
16. Curves in
17. Opposite of high
18. Curves out

Down

2. Bounced-back sound
3. Straight-line beam of light
5. Part of a sound wave where molecules are spread apart
7. Opposite of out
8. A noise
12. Blocks light going through
15. "Picture" of a light source

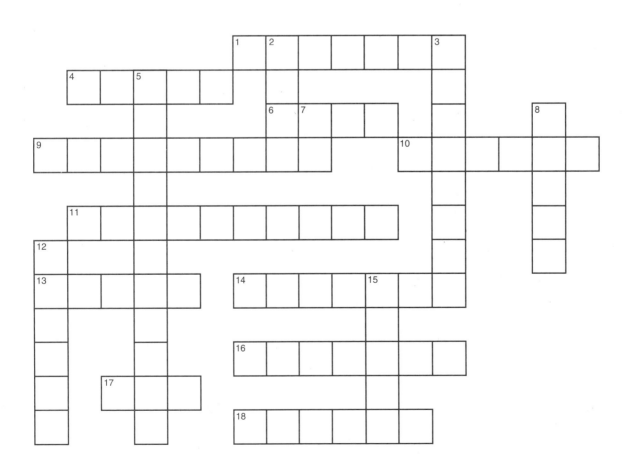

Find-a-Word

Look across, down, and diagonally to find these hidden words:

ABSORPTION, BLUE, COLOR, CONCAVE, CONVEX, CURVED, CYAN, DECIBEL, EAR, ECHO, ENERGY, EYE, FREQUENCY, GREEN, HEAR, HERTZ, HIGH, IMAGE, LASER, LENS, LOUD, LOW, OPAQUE, PHOTON, PIGMENT, PITCH, PRISM, RAREFACTION, RAY, RED, REFLECTION, SOFT, SOUND, SPECTRUM, TRANSLUCENT, ULTRASONIC, VACUUM, VIBRATION.

R	E	F	L	E	C	T	I	O	N	E	A	R	U
R	A	Y	A	C	O	G	Q	P	R	I	S	M	L
C	L	R	S	H	L	R	V	A	C	U	U	M	T
U	O	Z	E	O	O	E	Z	Q	B	L	U	E	R
R	W	X	R	F	R	E	Q	U	E	N	C	Y	A
V	H	I	G	H	A	N	L	E	N	S	Z	E	S
E	I	M	A	G	E	C	O	N	C	A	V	E	O
D	A	B	S	O	R	P	T	I	O	N	Z	S	N
P	E	Z	R	E	D	Z	P	I	T	C	H	P	I
I	S	C	Y	A	N	Q	H	Q	O	O	E	E	C
G	O	H	I	Q	T	S	O	F	T	N	N	C	H
M	U	E	Z	B	Z	I	T	X	Z	V	E	T	E
E	N	A	X	F	E	L	O	U	D	E	R	R	R
N	D	R	J	Q	X	L	N	N	X	X	G	U	T
T	R	A	N	S	L	U	C	E	N	T	Y	M	Z